FOR

DUMMIES®

PORTABLE EDITION

by **Edward C. Baig**

USA TODAY Personal Tech Columnist

and

Bob LeVitus

Houston Chronicle "Dr. Mac" Columnist

WILEY

John Wiley & Sons, Inc.

iPad® For Dummies®, Portable Edition

Published by
John Wiley & Sons, Inc.
111 River Street
Hoboken, NJ 07030-5774

www.wiley.com

Copyright © 2013 by John Wiley & Sons, Inc., Hoboken, New Jersey

Published by John Wiley & Sons, Inc., Hoboken, New Jersey

Published simultaneously in Canada

For general information on our other products and services, please contact our Customer Care Department within the U.S. at 877-762-2974, outside the U.S. at 317-572-3993, or fax 317-572-4002.

For technical support, please visit www.wiley.com/techsupport.

Wiley publishes in a variety of print and electronic formats and by print-on-demand. Some material included with standard print versions of this book may not be included in e-books or in print-on-demand. If this book refers to media such as a CD or DVD that is not included in the version you purchased, you may download this material at http://booksupport.wiley.com. For more information about Wiley products, visit www.wiley.com.

ISBN 978-1-118-37905-9 (pbk); ISBN 978-1-118-43652-3 (ebk); ISBN 978-1-118-43674-5 (ebk); ISBN 978-1-118-43677-6 (ebk)

Manufactured in the United States of America

10 9 8 7 6 5 4 3 2

WILEY

Publisher's Acknowledgments

We're proud of this book; please send us your comments at http://dummies. custhelp.com. For other comments, please contact our Customer Care Department within the U.S. at 877-762-2974, outside the U.S. at 317-572-3993, or fax 317-572-4002.

Some of the people who helped bring this book to market include the following:

Acquisitions and Editorial

Sr. Project Editor: Rebecca Huehls

Executive Editor: Bob Woerner

Technical Editor: Mark Chambers

Sr. Editorial Manager: Leah Cameron

Composition Services

Sr. Project Coordinator: Kristie Rees

Layout and Graphics: Jennifer Creasey

Proofreader: Tricia Liebig

Indexer: Potomac Indexing, LLC

Publishing and Editorial for Technology Dummies

    Richard Swadley, Vice President and Executive Group Publisher

    Andy Cummings, Vice President and Publisher

    Mary Bednarek, Executive Acquisitions Director

    Mary C. Corder, Editorial Director

Publishing for Consumer Dummies

    Kathleen Nebenhaus, Vice President and Executive Publisher

Composition Services

    Debbie Stailey, Director of Composition Services

Table of Contents

Introduction

*A*s Yogi Berra would say, "It was déjà vu all over again": Front-page treatment, top billing on network TV and cable, and diehards lining up days in advance to ensure landing a highly lusted-after product from Apple. Only this time around, the product generating the remarkable buzz wasn't the iPhone or even the latest Mac computer. It was the fourth-generation iPad and iPad mini. We trust you didn't pick up this book to read yet another account about how the latest iPad launch was an epochal event. We trust you *did* buy the book to find out how to get the very most out of your remarkable device, and that goes for any model of the iPad you may have newly acquired. Our goal is to deliver that information in a light and breezy fashion. We expect you to have fun using your iPad. We equally hope that you have fun spending time with us.

About This Book

We think you're pretty darn smart for buying a *For Dummies* book. That says to us that you have the confidence and intelligence to know what you don't know. The *For Dummies* franchise is built around the notion that everyone feels insecure about certain topics when tackling them for the first time, especially technical topics.

As with most Apple products, iPads are beautifully designed and intuitive to use. And though our editors may not want us to reveal this dirty little secret (especially on the first page), the truth is you'll get pretty far just by exploring the iPad's many functions and features on your own, without the help of this (or any other) book.

Now that we spilled the beans, please don't run back to the bookstore and request a refund. Why? This book is chock-full of useful tips, advice, and other nuggets that should make your iPad experience all the more pleasurable. We'd even go so far as to say you won't find some of these nuggets anywhere else. So keep this book nearby and consult it often.

Icons Used in This Book

Little round pictures (or *icons*) appear in the left margins throughout this book to tell you something extra about the topic at hand or hammer a point home. Here's what the four icons used in this book look like and mean.

These juicy morsels, shortcuts, and recommendations might make the task at hand faster or easier.

This icon emphasizes the stuff we think you ought to retain. You may even jot a note to yourself in the iPad.

Put on your propeller beanie hat and pocket protector; this text includes the truly geeky stuff. You can safely ignore this material, but if it weren't interesting or informative, we wouldn't have bothered to write it.

Ignoring warnings may be hazardous to your iPad and (by extension) your wallet. You now know how these warning icons work, for you have just received your first warning!

Where to Go from Here

Why straight to Chapter 1, of course (without passing Go). We want to thank you for buying our book. Please enjoy it along with your new iPad.

Note: At the time we wrote this book, all the information it contained was accurate for the Wi-Fi and Wi-Fi + 3/4G iPad, version 6 of the iOS (operating system) used by the iPad, and version 10.7 of iTunes. Apple is likely to introduce new versions of iOS and iTunes — and possibly even a new iPad device — between book editions. If your new iPad or the way it works look a little different from what you find in this book, check what Apple has to say about its latest releases at www.apple.com/ipad. When a change is very substantial, we may add an update or bonus information that you can download at this book's companion website, www.dummies.com/go/ipadfdupdates.

Chapter 1
Getting to Know Your iPad

In This Chapter

▷ Turning the device on and off and locking it

▷ Looking at the big picture

▷ Touring the outside of the iPad

▷ Discovering the stupendous Home screen

*C*ongratulations! You've selected one of the most incredible handheld devices we've ever seen. The iPad is a combination of a killer audio and video iPod, an e-book reader, a powerful Internet communications device, a movie and still camera, a video chat terminal, a superb handheld gaming device, and a platform for more than 300,000 apps (probably a lot more by the time you read this).

In this chapter, we offer a gentle introduction to all the pieces that make up your iPad, plus overviews of its revolutionary hardware and software features.

Turning the iPad On and Off

Apple has taken the time to partially charge your iPad, so you get some measure of instant gratification. After taking it out of the box, press and hold the Sleep/Wake button on the upper-right edge. At first, you see the famous Apple logo, followed a few seconds later by a connection symbol (the USB cable leading to an iTunes icon). This is your cue to sync your iPad, which we cover later, in Chapter 3.

To turn the device completely off, press and hold the Sleep/ Wake button again until a red arrow appears at the top of the screen. Then drag the arrow from the left to the right with your finger. Tap Cancel at the bottom of the screen if you change your mind.

Locking the iPad

Here are some sound reasons for locking your iPad:

- You can't inadvertently turn it on.
- You keep prying eyes at bay.
- You spare the battery some juice.

Apple makes it a cinch to lock the iPad.

In fact, you don't need to do anything to lock the iPad; by default, it happens automatically as long as you don't touch the screen for a minute or two. You can change this delay time from the General pane of the Settings screen (more about the Settings screen appears in later chapters).

Can't wait? To lock the iPad immediately, press the Sleep/ Wake button.

Unlocking the iPad is easy, too. Here's how it works:

1. **Press the Sleep/Wake button. Or press the Home button on the front of the screen.**

    Either way, the onscreen slider appears.

2. **Drag the slider to the right with your finger.**

3. **In some cases, you also need to enter a passcode.**

Even though your iPad is locked, you can still invoke Siri and give her voice commands — and you can drag the camera icon up to take photos or video. (More on both these nifty features later in the book.)

Exploring the iPad's Big Picture

The iPad has many best-of-class features, but perhaps its most unusual feature is the lack of a physical keyboard or stylus. Instead, it has a high-resolution touchscreen that you operate with your finger.

Another feature that knocks our socks off is the iPad's built-in sensors. An accelerometer detects when you rotate the device from portrait to landscape mode and instantly adjusts what's on the display accordingly.

A light sensor adjusts the display's brightness in response to the current ambient lighting conditions.

In the following sections, we're not just gawking over the wonderful screen. We take a brief look at some of the iPad's features, broken down by product category.

The iPad as an iPod

The iPad is magical — and without a doubt, the best iPod Apple has ever produced. You can enjoy all your existing iPod content — music, audiobooks, audio and video podcasts, music videos, television shows, and movies — on the iPad's gorgeous high-resolution color display, which is bigger, brighter, and richer than any iPad, iPod, or iPhone display that came before it.

Bottom line: If you can get the content — video, audio, or whatever — into iTunes on your Mac or PC, you can synchronize it and watch or listen to it on your iPad.

Chapter 3 is all about syncing; for now, just know that some video content may need to be converted to an iPad-compatible format (with proper resolution, frame rate, bit rate, and file format) to play on your iPad. If you try to sync an incompatible video file, iTunes will alert you that there's an issue. (Naturally, if you share movies from iMovie or images and video clips from iPhoto on your Mac and specify that the destination device is your iPad, Apple's applications will do the conversion chores automatically.)

If you get an error message about an incompatible video file, select the file in iTunes on your computer and choose Advanced⇨Create iPad or AppleTV Version. When the conversion is finished, sync again. Chapter 5 covers video in more detail.

The iPad as an Internet communications device

But wait — there's more! Not only is the iPad a stellar iPod, but it's also a full-featured Internet communications device with a rich HTML e-mail client that's compatible with most POP and IMAP mail services, with support for Microsoft Exchange ActiveSync. Also on-board is a world-class web browser (Safari) that, unlike on many mobile devices, makes web surfing fun and easy on the eyes. Chapter 4 explains how to surf the web using Safari.

There's been a lot of buzz about the iPad's built-in FaceTime application, and no wonder — it enables you to chat with another FaceTime user over a Wi-Fi or cellular Internet connection, complete with audio and real-time video! We cover FaceTime in Chapter 5.

You'll also find details about Message, the 3G/4G/Wi-Fi messaging app, in Chapter 4 — send unlimited photos, videos, and contacts as well as text to any iOS 5 (or later) device (along with the traditional SMS/MMS messages from your cellular carrier, if you have a 3G- or 4G-equipped iPad).

iOS 5 even integrates both Twitter and Facebook into many of your favorite apps, including Safari, Camera, Maps, and Videos!

Another cool Internet feature is Maps, a killer mapping application that's all-new in iOS 6. By using GPS (Wi-Fi + 3G/4G model) or triangulation (Wi-Fi model), the iPad can determine your location, let you view maps and satellite imagery, and obtain driving directions and traffic information regardless of where you happen to be. You can also find businesses such as gas stations, restaurants, hospitals, and Apple stores with just a few taps.

iOS 6 also finally delivers Siri to your iPad if you have the third- or fourth-generation model or an iPad mini. With a Wi-Fi or cellular data connection, your voice assistant can answer questions, run apps, play music, and even compose e-mail and text messages — all from commands that you speak. Siri is intelligent, helpful, and yes, she can tell jokes too.

The iPad as an e-book reader

Download the free iBooks app from the App Store, and you'll discover a completely new way of finding and reading books. The iBookstore, covered in Chapter 5, is chock full of good reading at prices that are lower than a hardcover copy. And best of all, a great number of books are absolutely free. If you've never read a book on your iPad, try it. We think you'll love it.

You can also use Newsstand, the central storage spot for all your magazine and newspaper application subscriptions. You'll find out more about Newsstand in Chapter 5.

The iPad as a platform for third-party apps

More than 300,000 iPad apps are available at this writing, in categories that include games, business, education, entertainment, healthcare and fitness, music, photography, productivity, travel, sports, and many more. The cool thing is that most of those iPhone apps run flawlessly on the iPad. Meanwhile, the App Store offers more than 75,000 apps designed specifically for the iPad's larger Retina screen, with many more on the way. Chapter 6 helps you fill your iPad with all the cool apps your heart desires.

What do you need to use your iPad?

To actually *use* your iPad, only a few simple things are required. Here is a list of everything you need:

✔ Any model of iPad (running iOS 6, if you want to take advantage of most of the new features covered in this book). The available models are the original iPad, iPad 2, third-generation iPad, fourth-generation iPad, and iPad mini.

✔ An Apple ID (assuming you want to acquire apps and digital media, as well as use iCloud)

✔ Internet access — broadband wireless Internet access recommended

Plus, if you want to sync your iPad with iTunes on your computer, you need *one* of the following:

✔ A Mac with a USB 2.0 port, OS X Mountain Lion version 10.8 or later, and iTunes 10.7 or later

✔ A PC with a USB 2.0 port; Windows 7, Windows Vista, or Windows XP Home or Professional with Service Pack 3 or later; and iTunes 10.7 or later

Touring the iPad Exterior

The iPad is a harmonious combination of hardware and software. The following sections look at the hardware — what's on the outside.

On the top edge

On the top of your iPad, you'll find the headphone jack and the Sleep/Wake button, as shown in Figure 1-1:

✔ **On/Off, Sleep/Wake button:** Use this button to put your iPad's screen to sleep or to wake it up. It's also how you turn your iPad on or off. To put it to sleep or wake it up, just press the button. To turn it on or off, press and hold the button for a few seconds.

Your iPad's battery runs down faster when your iPad is awake, so we suggest that you make a habit of putting it to sleep when you're not using it.

When your iPad is sleeping, nothing happens if you touch its screen. To wake it up, merely press the button again or press the Home button on the front of the device (as described in a moment).

Headphone jack: This jack lets you plug in a headset. You can use the Apple headsets or headphones that came with your iPhone or iPod. Or you can use pretty much any headphone or headset that plugs into a 3.5-mm stereo headphone jack.

Throughout this book, we use the words *headphones, earphones,* and *headset* interchangeably. Strictly speaking, a headset includes a microphone so that you can talk (or record) as well as listen; headphones or earphones are for listening only. Either type works with your iPad.

Microphone: This tiny dot is actually a pretty good microphone. The newer iPad models even offer voice dictation, which we cover in Chapter 2.

Although your iPad doesn't include the Voice Notes app that comes with the iPhone, the App Store offers several free voice-recording apps for the iPad and/or iPhone.

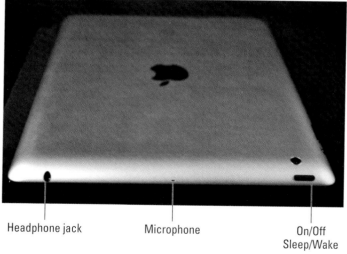

Headphone jack   Microphone   On/Off
                                                      Sleep/Wake

Figure 1-1: The top edge of the iPad.

On the bottom edge

On the bottom of your iPad are the speaker and the dock connector, as shown in Figure 1-2:

✔ **Speaker:** The speaker plays audio — music or video soundtracks — if no headset is plugged in.

✔ **Dock connector:** This connector has two purposes. One, you can use it to recharge your iPad's battery: Simply connect one end of the included dock connector–to–USB cable to the dock connector and the other end to the USB power adapter. Two, you can use the dock connector to synchronize your iPad with your computer: Connect one end of the same cable to the dock connector and the other end to a USB port on your Mac or PC. (Note that your iPad's battery also recharges while it's connected to your computer, but much more slowly. For the shortest charging times, use your USB power adapter.) Older iPad models, like the iPad 2 shown in Figure 1-2, have a 30-pin dock connector. The new fourth-generation iPad and iPad mini use a new, smaller Lightning connector as the dock connector.

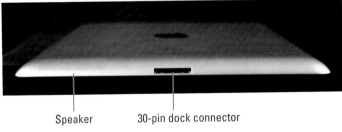

Speaker   30-pin dock connector

Figure 1-2: The bottom edge of the iPad.

On the sides, front, and back

The right edge of your iPad has the Volume Up/Down control and Side switch, as shown in Figure 1-3:

✔ **Side switch:** You can set this switch as either a silent switch or a screen rotation lock from within the Settings app. (The exception is the very first iPad model.) When configured as a silent switch and set to silent mode — the down position, with an orange dot visible on the switch — your iPad doesn't make any sound when you receive new mail or an alert pops up on the screen. However, it doesn't silence the iTunes or Videos apps, nor does it mute games and other apps that include noises. When set as a screen rotation lock, the side switch prevents your screen orientation from changing when you rotate your iPad.

To change the function of the side switch, from the Home screen, tap Settings⟳General⟳Use Side Switch to Mute or Use Side Switch to Lock Rotation.

✔ **Volume Up/Down control:** The Volume Up/Down control is a single button that's just below the screen rotation lock. The upper part of the button increases the volume; the lower part decreases it.

Volume Up/Down

Side switch

Back camera

Figure 1-3: Right-side view of the iPad.

If you're using an iPad with 3G/4G hardware, you may see a Micro-SIM card tray on the left side of the device. This tray is used to install a Micro-SIM card from your cellular provider.

On the front of your iPad, you find the following (labeled in Figure 1-4):

✔ **Front camera:** Your iPad sports not one but two camera lenses — this one faces forward, allowing two-way video chatting in FaceTime. (The exception is the first iPad model.) More about FaceTime in Chapter 5.

✔ **Touchscreen:** You find out how to use the iPad's gorgeous high-resolution color touchscreen in Chapter 2. All we have to say at this time is . . . try not to drool all over it.

✓ **Home button:** No matter what you're doing, you can press the Home button at any time to display the Home screen, as shown in Figure 1-4.

✓ **Application buttons:** Each button (icon) shown on the screen in Figure 1-4 launches an included iPad application. You read more about these applications later in this chapter and throughout the rest of the book.

On the back of your iPad, in the top-left corner, you'll find another camera lens for taking video and still photos — this camera delivers better quality than the front camera.

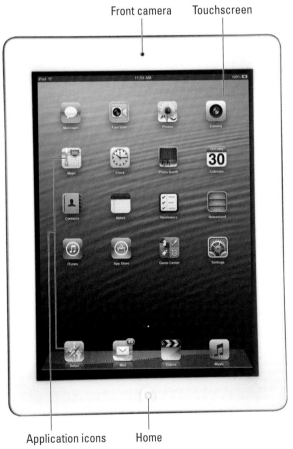

Front camera   Touchscreen

Application icons   Home

Figure 1-4: The front of the iPad is a study in simplicity.

Status bar

The status bar, which is at the top of the screen, displays tiny icons that provide a variety of information about the current state of your iPad:

Airplane mode (Wi-Fi + 3G/4G models only): You're allowed to use your iPod on a plane after the captain gives the word. But you can't use a cell phone or iPad Wi-Fi + 3G/4G except when the plane is in the gate area before takeoff or after landing. Fortunately, your iPad offers an airplane mode, which turns off all wireless features of your iPad — the cellular, 3G, 4G, 4G LTE, General Packet Radio Service (GPRS), and EDGE networks; Wi-Fi; and Bluetooth — and makes it possible to enjoy music or video during your flight.

3G 3G (Wi-Fi + 3G/4G models only): This icon informs you that the high-speed 3G data network from your wireless carrier (that's AT&T or Verizon in the United States) is available and that your iPad can connect to the Internet via 3G.

4G 4G (Wi-Fi + 4G models only): This icon indicates that a 4G data network is available from AT&T or Verizon (in the United States) and that your iPad can connect to the Internet via 4G.

LTE LTE (Wi-Fi + 4G models only): This icon tells you that a 4G LTE data network is available from AT&T or Verizon (in the United States) and that your iPad can connect to the Internet via 4G LTE.

GPRS (Wi-Fi + 3G/4G models only): This icon says that your wireless carrier's GPRS data network is available and that your iPad can use it to connect to the Internet.

E EDGE (Wi-Fi + 3G/4G models only): This icon tells you that your wireless carrier's EDGE network is available and you can use it to connect to the Internet.

Wi-Fi: If you see the Wi-Fi icon, it means your iPad is connected to the Internet over a Wi-Fi network. The more semicircular lines you see (up to three), the stronger the Wi-Fi signal. If you have only one or two semicircles of Wi-Fi strength, try moving around a bit. If you don't see the Wi-Fi icon in the status bar, Internet access is not currently available.

Syncing: This icon indicates that your iPad is syncing with iTunes on your Mac or PC over a USB cable connection.

Personal Hotspot: This icon informs you that your iPad is operating as a Wi-Fi bridge (or hotspot) to provide other iOS devices, Macs, and PCs with a shared Internet connection. (You must arrange for this feature with your cellular carrier, and it generally costs an additional fee to use.)

Activity: This icon tells you that some network or other activity is occurring, such as over-the-air synchronization, sending or receiving e-mail, or loading a web page. Some third-party applications also use this icon to indicate network or other activity.

VPN: This icon shows that you are currently connected to a virtual private network (VPN).

Lock: This icon tells you when your iPad is locked, as we mention earlier in this chapter.

Play: This icon informs you that a song is currently playing. You find out more about playing songs in Chapter 5.

Bluetooth: This icon indicates the current state of your iPad's Bluetooth connection. If you see this icon in the status bar, Bluetooth is on, and a device (such as a wireless headset or keyboard) is connected. If the icon is gray (as shown on the right in the picture in the margin), Bluetooth is turned on, but no device is connected. If the icon is white (as shown on the left in the picture in the margin), Bluetooth is on, and one or more devices is connected. If you don't see a Bluetooth icon at all, Bluetooth is turned off.

Screen rotation lock: This icon appears when the Screen Rotation Lock is engaged.

Battery: This icon reflects the level of your battery's charge. It's completely filled when you are not connected to a power source and your battery is fully charged (as shown in the margin). It then empties as your battery becomes depleted. The icon shows when you're connected to a power source, and when the battery is fully charged or currently charging. You see an onscreen message when the charge drops to 20% or below and another when it reaches 10%.

If you've enabled Location Services within Settings, your iPad will display an arrow-shaped pointer to indicate that an app is reading your current location.

The iPad's Stupendous Home Screen Icons

The Home screen offers 20 icons by default, each representing a different built-in application or function. We provide brief descriptions here.

To get to your Home screen, tap the Home button (refer to Figure 1-4). If your iPad is asleep when you tap, the unlock screen appears. After it is unlocked, you see whichever page of icons was on the screen when it went to sleep. If that happens to have been the Home screen, you're golden. If it wasn't, merely tap the Home button again to summon your iPad's Home screen.

Three steps let you rearrange icons on your iPad:

1. **Press and hold any icon until all the icons begin to "wiggle."**

2. **Drag the icons around until you're happy with their positions.**

3. **Press the Home button to save your arrangement and stop the "wiggling."**

If you haven't rearranged your icons, you see the following applications on your Home screen, starting at the top left:

✔ **Messages:** Send and receive unlimited messages with any Mac or iOS 5 (or later) device, including the iPhone and iPod touch. Your messages can include photos, video, contacts, and current locations. Chapter 4 explains more about Messages.

✔ **FaceTime:** Tap this icon to start a two-way video chat with a Mac computer, another iPad, an iPod touch, or an iPhone 4/4S/5. Just remember that to use FaceTime, both your iPad and your friend's device must have a camera and the FaceTime app.

✔ **Photos:** This application is the iPad's terrific photo manager. You can view pictures that you've taken (with your iPad) or transferred from your computer, camera, or SD card reader (using the optional Camera Connection Kit). iCloud can deliver new photos wirelessly from your Mac's iPhoto library using Photo Stream, or to Shared Photo Streams that distribute your photos only to contacts you specify. You can zoom in or out, create slideshows, e-mail photos to friends, and much more.

✔ **Camera:** This icon opens the iPad Camera application, which lets you take still photographs and video clips.

✔ **Maps:** This application is among our favorites. View street maps or satellite imagery of locations around the globe, or ask for directions, traffic conditions, or even the location of a nearby pizza joint.

✔ **Clock:** View the time in multiple time zones, and set alarms for those early meetings.

✔ **Photo Booth:** Remember the coin-operated photo booth at arcades and carnivals? This app enables you to take photos with all sorts of special effects (favorites are Thermal Camera and Squeeze). The perfect party app!

✔ **Calendar:** No matter what calendar program you prefer on your PC or Mac (as long as it's Calendar, Microsoft Entourage, or Microsoft Outlook), you can synchronize events and alerts between your computer and your iPad.

✔ **Contacts:** This handy app contains information about the people you know. Like the Calendar app, it synchronizes with the Contacts application on your Mac or PC (as long as it's Contacts, Microsoft Entourage, or Microsoft Outlook), and you can synchronize contacts between your computer and your iPad.

✔ **Notes:** This program enables you to type notes while you're out and about. You can send the notes to yourself or to anyone else through e-mail, allow them to sync over iCloud, or just save them on your iPad until you need them.

✔ **Reminders:** This app makes it easy to organize your time by setting to-do lists, complete with reminders that are updated automatically across all your devices and Mac computers. Reminders can even be triggered by your arrival at a specific location.

✔ **Newsstand:** Peruse your newspaper and magazine subscriptions, automatically updated of course!

✔ **iTunes:** Tap this puppy to purchase music, movies, TV shows, audiobooks, and more.

✔ **App Store:** This icon enables you to connect to and search the App Store for iPad applications that you can purchase or download free over a Wi-Fi or cellular data network connection.

✔ **Game Center:** This is Apple's social networking app for game enthusiasts. Compare achievements, boast of your conquests and high scores, or challenge your friends to battle.

✔ **Settings:** This is where you change settings for your iPad and its apps.

✔ **Safari:** Safari is your web browser. If you're a Mac user, you know that already. If you're a Windows user who hasn't already discovered the wonderful Safari for Windows, think Internet Explorer on steroids.

✔ **Mail:** This application enables you to send and receive e-mail with most POP3 and IMAP e-mail systems and, if you work for a company that grants permission, Microsoft Exchange, too.

✔ **Videos:** This handy app is the repository for your movies, TV shows, and music videos. You add videos via iTunes on your Mac or PC, or by purchasing them from the iTunes Store using the iTunes app on your iPad.

✔ **Music:** Last but not least, this icon unleashes all the power of an iPod right on your iPad, so you can listen to music, audiobooks, or podcasts.

Chapter 2
Mastering Multitouch

*I*f you already own an iPhone or its close relative, Apple's iPod touch, you have a gigantic start in mastering the iPad multitouch method of navigating the interface with your fingers. You have our permission to skim over the rest of this chapter, although we urge you to stick around anyway because some things on the iPad work in subtly different ways. If you're a total novice, don't fret. Nothing about multitouch is painful.

With very few exceptions, until the original iPad came along, almost every computer known to humanity has had a physical mouse and a typewriter-style QWERTY keyboard to help you accomplish most of the things you can do on a computer.

The iPad, like the iPhone, dispenses with a physical mouse (or trackpad) and keyboard. Apple is once again living up to an old company advertising slogan to "Think Different."

Indeed, the iPad (and iPhone) remove the usual physical buttons in favor of a *multitouch display.* And this beautiful and responsive finger-controlled screen is at the heart of the many things you do on the iPad. In the following sections, you discover how to move around the multitouch interface with ease. You also find a quick introduction to Siri, Apple's voice-activated personal digital assistant, which you can use when you don't want to use your fingers at all.

Training Your Digits

Rice Krispies have Snap! Crackle! Pop! Apple's response for the iPad is Tap! Flick! and Pinch! Oh yeah, and drag.

Fortunately, tapping, flicking, pinching, and dragging are not challenging gestures, so you can master many of these features in no time:

- **Tap:** This action serves multiple purposes. Tap an icon to open an application from the Home screen. Tap to start playing a song or to choose the photo album you want to look through. Sometimes, you double-tap (tapping twice in rapid succession), which has the effect of zooming in (or out) of web pages, maps, and e-mails.

- **Flick:** This action is just what it sounds like. A flick of the finger on the screen itself lets you quickly scroll through lists of songs, e-mails, and picture thumbnails. Tap on the screen to stop scrolling, or merely wait for the scrolling list to stop.

- **Swipe:** Swipe downward from the top of the screen — all it takes is one finger — and your iPhone displays the Notification Center, where you can track all notifications you receive (including calls and voicemails, messages displayed by apps, and even weather and stock figures). Many apps also enable you to browse photos and screens by swiping left and right across your screen.

- **Pinch/spread:** Place two fingers on the edges of a web page or map or picture, and then spread your fingers apart to enlarge the images. Or, pinch your fingers together to make the map or picture smaller. Pinching and spreading (or what we call *unpinching*) are cool gestures that are easy to master and sure to wow an audience.

- **Drag:** Here's where you slowly press your finger against the touchscreen without lifting it. You might drag to move around a web page or map that's too large for the iPad's display area.

Navigating Beyond Home

The Home screen (refer to Chapter 1) is not the only screen of icons on your tablet. After you start adding apps from the App Store (on your iPad) or the iTunes App Store (on your computer, which you discover in Chapter 6), you may see two or more tiny dots between the Safari, Mail, Videos, and Music icons and the row of icons directly above them, plus a tiny Spotlight search magnifying glass to the left of the dots. Those dots denote additional screens, each containing up to 20 additional icons, not counting the 4 to 6 separate icons that are docked at the bottom of each of these screens. (More on these in a moment.)

To navigate between screens, either flick your finger from right to left or left to right across the middle of the screen, or tap directly on the dots. You can also drag your finger in either horizontal direction to get to a different screen.

Unlike flicking or swiping, dragging your finger means keeping it pressed against the screen until you get to the page you want.

You must be very precise, or you'll open one of the application icons instead of switching screens.

The number of dots you see represents the current number of screens on your iPad. The dot that's all white denotes the screen you're currently viewing. Finally, the four icons in the bottom row — Safari, Mail, Videos, and Music — are in a special part of the screen known as the *dock*. When you switch from screen to screen as we described earlier, these icons remain on the screen. In other words, only the first 20 icons on the screen change when you move from one screen to another. You can add one or two more icons to the dock if you so choose. Or move one of the four default icons into the main area of the Home screen to make space available for additional app icons you may use more often.

Press the Home button to jump back to the Home screen.

Here's another multitouch gesture introduced with iOS 5: If you've populated your iPad with several screens of apps, you can also pinch on the background to return to the Home screen.

The Incredible, Intelligent, and Virtual Keyboard

Instead of a physical keyboard, several "soft" or "virtual" English-language keyboard layouts slide up from the bottom of the iPad screen, all variations on the alphabetical keyboard, the numeric and punctuation keyboard, and the more punctuation and symbols keyboard. Figure 2-1 shows the three most common examples of iPad keyboards.

Figure 2-1: Three faces of the iPad keyboard.

Indeed, the beauty of a software keyboard is that you see only the keys that are pertinent to the task at hand. The layout you see depends on the application. The keyboards in Safari differ from the keyboards in Notes. For example, while having a dedicated *.com* key in the Safari keyboard makes perfect sense, having such a key in the Notes keyboard isn't essential.

Before you consider how to actually *use* the keyboard, we'd like to share a bit of the philosophy behind its so-called *intelligence.* Knowing what makes this keyboard smart can help you make it even smarter when you use it:

- It has a built-in English dictionary that even includes words from today's popular culture. It has dictionaries in other languages, too, automatically activated when you use a given international keyboard.

- It adds your contacts to its dictionary automatically.

- It uses complex analysis algorithms to predict the word you're trying to type.

- It suggests corrections as you type. It then offers you the suggested word just below the misspelled word. When you decline a suggestion and the word you typed is *not* in the iPad dictionary, the iPad adds that word to its dictionary and offers it as a suggestion if you mistype a similar word in the future.

Remember to *decline* suggestions (by tapping the characters you typed as opposed to the suggested words that appear beneath what you've typed) because doing so helps your intelligent keyboard become even smarter.

- It reduces the number of mistakes you make as you type by intelligently and dynamically resizing the touch zones for certain keys. You can't see it, but it is increasing the zones for keys it predicts might come next and decreasing the zones for keys that are unlikely or impossible to come next.

Discovering the special-use keys

The iPad keyboard contains several keys that don't actually type a character. Here's the scoop on each of these keys:

 Shift: If you're using the alphabetical keyboard, the Shift key (arrow pointing up) switches between uppercase and lowercase letters. You can tap the key to change the case, or hold down Shift and slide to the letter you want to be capitalized.

#+= or 123: If you're using keyboards that just show numbers and symbols, the traditional Shift key is replaced by a key labeled #+= or 123 (sometimes shown as .?123). Pressing that key toggles between keyboards that just have symbols and numbers. Press the ABC key to return to the alphabetical keyboard.

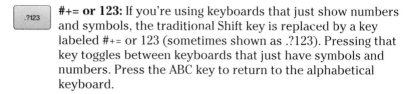

Caps Lock: To turn on Caps Lock and type in all caps, you first need to enable Caps Lock (if not already enabled). To do so, from the Home screen, tap Settings⟳General⟳Keyboard. Tap the Enable Caps Lock item to turn it on. After the Caps Lock setting is enabled, double-tap the Shift key to turn on Caps Lock. (The Shift key turns blue whenever Caps Lock is on.) Tap the Shift key again to turn off Caps Lock. To disable Caps Lock completely, just reverse the process by turning off the Enable Caps Lock setting (tap Settings⟳General⟳Keyboard).

International Keyboard: Only shows up if you've turned on an international keyboard.

Dictation: One of the features introduced within iOS 5.1 was *dictation*, which enables you to speak the text of a Mail message, the body of a Note, or the text of an iMessage. (Note that your iPad must have an Internet connection to use dictation.) When the Dictation key (which looks like a microphone) appears, tap it and begin speaking — you'll note that the Dictation key expands to display the audio level while you're talking (Figure 2-2), which can indicate that you need to speak up in an especially noisy environment. When you've finished dictating, tap the Dictation key again. You can add punctuation marks within your text by speaking them — for example, "exclamation point" and "comma".

Delete: Otherwise known as Backspace, tapping this key erases the character immediately to the left of the cursor.

Return: Moves the cursor to the beginning of the next line.

Hide Keyboard: This icon looks like a tiny keyboard on top of a down arrow. Tap it to hide the keyboard. Tap the screen in the appropriate app to bring back the keyboard.

Figure 2-2: Preparing to dictate text to the iPad.

 If you have an iPhone or iPod touch, it's worth noting that keyboards on the iPad more closely resemble the keyboard layout of a traditional computer rather than those smaller devices. That is, the Backspace space key is on the upper right, the Return key is just below it, and there are Shift keys on either side. The more-computer-like keyboard layout certainly improves the odds of successful touch-typing.

Finger-typing on the virtual keyboards

If you're patient and trusting, in a week or so, you'll get the hang of finger-typing — which is vital to moving forward, of course, because you rely on a virtual keyboard to tap a text field, enter notes, type the names of new contacts, and so on.

As we've already noted, Apple has built intelligence into its virtual keyboard, so it can correct typing mistakes on the fly and take a stab at predicting what you're about to type next. The keyboard isn't exactly Nostradamus, but it does an excellent job in coming up with the words you have in mind.

As you start typing on the virtual keyboard, we think you'll find the following tips extremely helpful:

> ✔ **See what letter you're typing.** As you press your finger against a letter or number on the screen, the individual key you press darkens until you lift your finger, as shown in Figure 2-3. That way, you know that you struck the correct letter or number.

Figure 2-3: The ABCs of virtual typing.

✔ **Slide to the correct letter if you tap the wrong one.** No need to worry if you touched the wrong key. You can slide your finger to the correct key because the letter isn't recorded until you release your finger.

✔ **Tap and hold to access special accent marks (or in Safari, web address endings).** Sending a message to an overseas pal? Keep your finger pressed against a letter, and a row of keys showing variations on the character for foreign alphabets pops up. This lets you add the appropriate accent mark. Just slide your finger until the key with the relevant accent mark is pressed.

Meanwhile, if you press and hold the .com key in Safari, it offers you the choice of .com, .net, .edu, or .org, with additional options if you also use international keyboards. Pretty slick stuff.

✔ **Tap the Space key to accept a suggested word, or tap the suggested word to decline the suggestion.** Alas, mistakes are common at first. Say that you meant to type a sentence in the Notes application that reads, "I am typing an important . . ." But because of the way your fingers struck the virtual keys, you actually entered "I am typing an *importsnt* . . ." Fortunately, Apple knows that the *a* you meant to press is next to the *s* that showed up on the keyboard, just as *t* and *y* and *e* and *r* are side by side. So the software determines that *important* was indeed the word you had in mind and places it in red under the suspect word. To accept the suggested word, merely tap the Space key. And if for some reason you actually did mean to type *importsnt* instead, tap on the word you typed to decline the suggestion.

If you don't appreciate this feature, you can turn off Auto-Correction in Settings. Turn to Chapter 7 for details.

Because Apple knows what you're up to, the virtual keyboard is fine-tuned for the task at hand. This is especially true when you need to enter numbers, punctuation, or symbols. The following tips help you find common special characters or special keys that we know you'll want to use:

✔ **Finding keys for web addresses:** If you're entering a web address, the keyboard inside the Safari web browser (Chapter 4) includes dedicated period, forward slash, and .com keys but no Space key.

If you're using the Notes application, the keyboard does have a Space key.

✔ **Putting the @ in an e-mail address:** And if you're composing an e-mail message (Chapter 4), a dedicated @ key pops up on the keyboard.

✔ **Switching from letters to numbers:** When you're typing notes or sending e-mail and want to type a number, symbol, or punctuation mark, tap the 123 key to bring up an alternative virtual keyboard. Tap the ABC key to return to the first keyboard. It's not hard to get used to, but some may find this extra step irritating.

✔ **Adding apostrophes:** If you press and hold the Exclamation Mark/Comma key on the iPad, it changes to an apostrophe.

Editing mistakes

It's a good idea to type with abandon and not get hung up over mistyped characters. The self-correcting keyboard can fix many errors. That said, plenty of typos are likely to turn up, especially in the beginning, and you have to correct them manually.

A neat trick for doing so is to hold your finger against the screen to bring up the magnifying glass shown in Figure 2-4. Use it to position the pointer to the spot where you need to make the correction. Then use the Backspace key to delete the error, and press whatever keys you need to type the correct text.

Figure 2-4: Magnifying errors while typing in Notes.

Select, cut, copy, and paste

Being able to select and then copy and paste from one place on a computer to another has seemingly been a divine right since Moses, and that's the case on the Apple tablet as well. You can copy and paste (and cut) with pizzazz.

On the iPad, you might copy text or images from the web and paste them into an e-mail or a note. Or you might copy a bunch of pictures or video into an e-mail.

Say you're jotting down ideas in the Notes application that you'll eventually copy into an e-mail. Here's how to exploit the copy-and-paste feature, using this scenario as an example:

1. **Tap a word to select it.**

2. **Tap Select to select the adjacent word or tap Select All to grab everything.**

   You can also drag the blue grab points or handles to select a larger block of text or to contract the text you've already selected. This, too, may take a little practice.

3. **After you select the text, tap Copy (see Figure 2-5). If you want to delete the text block, tap Cut instead.**

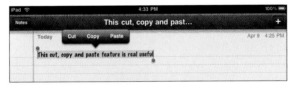

Figure 2-5: Drag the grab points to select text.

You can also select Replace to substitute for the words you've selected, or Define to display the dictionary definition for the word or phrase.

4. **Open the Mail program (discussed in Chapter 4) and start composing a message.**

5. **When you decide where to insert the text you just copied, tap the cursor.**

   Up pops commands to Select, Select All, and Paste, as shown in Figure 2-6.

Figure 2-6: Tap Paste to make text appear from nowhere.

6. Tap Paste to paste the text into the message.

Here's the pizzazz part. If you made a mistake when you were cutting, pasting, or typing, shake the iPad. It undoes the last edit.

Multitasking

iOS 6 software includes a bevy of important features, of which multitasking is arguably the most significant. *Multitasking* simply lets you run numerous apps in the background simultaneously or easily switch from one app to another. For example, a third-party app such as Slacker continues to play music while you surf the web, peek at pictures, or check e-mail. Without multitasking, Slacker would shut down the moment you opened another app. (Previously, Apple did let you multitask by, for example, playing audio in the background with its own Music app. But multitasking was limited to Apple's own apps, not those produced by outside developers.)

Among other tricks, the multitasking feature lets a navigation app update your position while you're listening, say, to Pandora Internet radio. From time to time, the navigation app will pipe in with turn-by-turn directions, lowering the volume of the music so you can hear the instructions.

And if you're uploading images to a photo website and the process is taking longer than you'd like, you can switch to another app, confident that the images will continue to upload behind the scenes. We've also been able to leave voice notes in the Evernote app while checking out a web page.

Multitasking couldn't be simpler. Double-press the Home button — or use the new gesture, swiping upward with four or five fingers — and a tray appears at the bottom of the screen, as shown in Figure 2-7. The tray holds icons for the most recently used apps. Swipe from right to left on the tray to see more apps. Tap the app you want to switch to; the app remembers where you left off.

Or swipe the tray from left to right for instant access to convenient controls for Music audio (Volume, Play/Pause, Next/ Previous Track), Brightness, and Screen Rotation Lock.

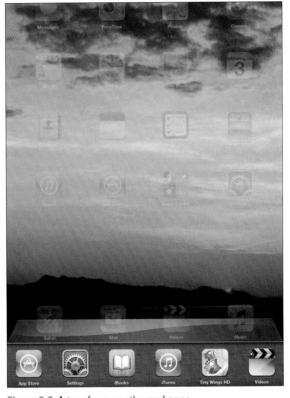

Figure 2-7: A tray for recently used apps.

To remove an app from the tray holding icons of the most recently used apps — and thus remove the app from those in the multitasking rotation — press and hold your finger against any app until they all start to wiggle. Then tap the red circle with the white line that appears inside the app you want to remove. *Poof!* It's gone.

Multitasking on the iPad differs from multitasking on a PC or a Mac. You can't display more than one screen at a time. Moreover, there's some philosophical debate whether this feature is multitasking, fast task switching, or a combination. Rather than getting bogged down in the semantics, we're just glad that multitasking, or whatever you want to call it, is here and convenient to use.

Organizing Icons into Folders

Finding the single app you want to use among apps spread out over 11 pages may seem like a daunting task. But Apple felt your pain and includes a handy organizational tool called Folders. The Folders feature lets you create folder icons, each with up to 20 icons for apps.

To create a folder, press your finger against an icon until all the icons on the screen jiggle. Decide which apps you want to move to a folder, and drag the icon for the first app on top of a second app. The apps now share living quarters inside a newly created folder, as shown in Figure 2-8. Apple names the folder according to the category of apps inside the folder, but you can easily change the folder name by tapping the X in the bar where the folder name appears and substituting a new name.

Figure 2-8: Dragging one app on top of another creates a folder.

To launch an app that's inside a folder, tap that folder's icon and then tap the icon for the app that you want to open.

You can drag apps into and out of any folder as long as there's room for them. When you drag all the apps from a folder, the folder disappears automatically.

Printing

With AirPrint, you can print wirelessly from the iPad to an AirPrint-capable printer. The first of these compatible printers emerged on a wide range of HP models, and a number of Canon Wi-Fi printers now offer the feature. The expectation is that other printer manufacturers will unveil AirPrint printers of their own perhaps by the time you read this. AirPrint works (as of this writing) with Mail, Photos, Safari, iBooks (PDFs), and third-party apps that include printing support. You can also print from apps in Apple's optional iWork software suite.

To print, tap the Print command, which appears in different places depending on the app you're using. Then tap Select Printer to select a printer, which the iPad should locate in short order. Depending on the printer, you can specify the number of copies you want to print, the number of double-sided copies, and a range of pages to print.

Although AirPrint printers don't need any special software, they do have to be connected to the same Wi-Fi network as the iPad.

If you happen to double-press the Home button while a print job is underway, the Print Center app icon appears on the multitasking tray along with all your other recently used apps. A red badge indicates how many documents are in the print queue, along with the currently printing document. Tap the Print Center icon to display additional information about the document that's currently printing, or to cancel the printing of the current document.

Searching for Content

Using the Safari browser (see Chapter 4), you can search the web via the Google or Yahoo! search engines.

But you can also search people and programs across your iPad and within specific applications. We show you how to search within apps in the various chapters dedicated to Mail, Contacts, Calendar, and the iPod.

Searching across the iPad, meanwhile, is based on the powerful Spotlight feature familiar to Mac owners. Here's how it works:

1. **To access Spotlight, flick to the left of the main Home screen.**

2. **In the bar at the top of the screen that slides into view, enter your search query using the virtual keyboard.**

   The iPad starts spitting out results the moment you type a single character, and the list narrows while you type additional characters.

   The results are pretty darn thorough. Say you entered **Ring** as your search term. Contacts whose last names have *Ring* in them show up, along with friends who might do a trapeze act in the Ringling Bros. circus. All the songs on your iPad by Ringo Starr show up too, as do such song titles as Tony Bennett's "When Do the Bells Ring for Me," if that happens to be in your library. Same goes for apps with the word *Ring*.

3. **Tap any listing to jump to the contact, tune, or application you're searching for.**

In Settings (see Chapter 7), you can specify the order of search results so that apps come first, contacts second, songs third, and so on. Within Settings, tap General➪Spotlight Search.

Summoning Siri

When your hands aren't available to type, check out Siri. The intelligent voice-activated virtual personal assistant has been living like a genie inside the iPhone 4S and iPhone 5, and now it arrives on the iPad! You find Siri on the third- and fourth-generation iPads and iPad mini. Siri not only *hear*s what you have to say but attempts to respond to your wishes. She — yes, it's a female voice, at least at the time of this writing — can help you dictate and send a message, get directions, call a friend, and more.

When you first set up the iPad under iOS 6, you have the option of turning on Siri. If you did so, you're good to go. If you didn't, tap Settings⇨General⇨Siri and flip the switch so that On is showing.

To call Siri into action, press and hold the Home button until you hear a tone and then start talking. Pretty simple, eh? At the bottom of the screen, you'll see a picture of a microphone inside a circle, as shown in Figure 2-9. The question, "What can I help you with?" appears on the screen.

Siri also responds when you press a button on a Bluetooth headset.

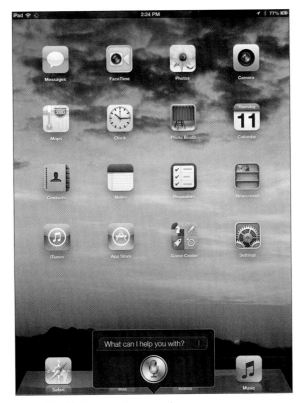

Figure 2-9: Siri is eager to respond.

What happens next is up to you. You can ask a wide range
of questions or issue voice commands. If you didn't get your
words out fast enough or Siri misunderstood you, tap the
microphone icon and try again.

Siri requires Internet access, either via Wi-Fi or your cellular
provider. A lot of factors go into its accuracy, including sur-
rounding noises and unfamiliar accents.

If you're not sure what to ask, tap the circled *i* to list sample
questions or commands, as shown in Figure 2-10. You can
actually tap on any of these examples to see even more
samples.

Figure 2-10: Siri can help out in many ways.

Here are some of the ways Siri can lend a hand, um, voice:

- **Music:** "Play Frank Sinatra."
- **Messages:** "Send a message to Nancy to reschedule lunch."
- **Calendar:** "Set up a meeting for 9 a.m. to discuss funding."
- **Reminders:** "Remind me to take my medicine at 8 a.m. tomorrow."
- **Maps:** "Find an ATM near here."
- **Mail:** "Mail the tenant about the recent check."
- **Stocks:** "What is the Dow at?"
- **Web search:** "Who was the 19th president of the United States?"
- **Movies:** "When is *The Hobbit* showing?"
- **WolframAlpha:** "How many calories are in a blueberry muffin?"
- **Sports:** "What's the score in the Cardinals game?"
- **Clock:** "Wake me up at 8:30 in the morning."

Voice isn't the solution to everything. Putting Siri to work typically involves a combination of using voice, touch, and your eyes to see what's on the screen.

As noted, you can call upon Siri even from the Lock screen. That's the default setting. Consider this feature a mixed blessing. Not having to type a passcode to get Siri to do her thing is convenient. But, if your iPad ends up with the wrong person, he or she would be able to use Siri to make a call, send an e-mail, or send a message in your name, bypassing whatever passcode security you thought was in place. To change the default behavior, tap Settings➪General➪Passcode Lock and enter your passcode to verify your identity. Within the Allow Access When Locked section, switch the Siri option from On to Off.

Chapter 3

Getting Stuff to and from Your iPad

*W*e have good news and . . . more good news. The good news is that you can easily copy any or all of your contacts, calendars, mail settings, bookmarks, books (both electronic and audio), music, movies, TV shows, podcasts, photos, and applications from your computer to your iPad. And the more good news is that all that data is kept up to date automatically in both places — on your computer and your iPad — whenever you make a change in one place or the other. So when you add or change a calendar or a contact on your iPad, that information automatically appears on your computer the next time your iPad and computer communicate (either wirelessly through iCloud or by using a USB cable connection). In the same manner, any apps, music, books, videos, or movies you purchase through the iTunes Store can be downloaded to your iPad automatically, or even re-downloaded (in case you have to reset your device).

This automatic wireless communication via iCloud between your iPad and computer is called *pushing*, but you can also transfer data the old-fashioned way: by *syncing* (short for synchronizing) using the USB cable that accompanied your iPad.

Don't worry: It's easy, and we're going to walk you through the entire process in this chapter.

We also introduce you to the Notification Center, which gathers all the notifications from your applications in one convenient, easy-to-use location.

The information in this chapter is based on iTunes version 10.7 and iOS 6, which were the latest and greatest when these words were written. If your screens don't look like ours, upgrade to iTunes 10.7 or higher (choose iTunes⬧Check for Update) and iOS 6 or higher (click the Check for Updates button on the Summary tab, discussed a little later, and follow the instructions for updating your iPad). By the way, both upgrades are free, and both offer significant advantages over their predecessors.

Starting to Sync

Synchronizing your iPad with your computer over a USB cable connection is a lot like syncing an iPod or iPhone with your computer. If you're an iPod or iPhone user, the process will be a familiar piece of cake. But it's not too difficult even for those who've never used an iPod, an iPhone, or iTunes. (Don't forget, many of the steps in the following process only occur the first time you sync your iPad — in fact, you may only need to sync using a cable once!)

First, make sure you've installed iTunes 10.7 (or later) on your Mac or PC (if you need to download it, visit www.apple.com/ipad for your own free copy). After you've installed iTunes, follow these steps:

1. **Connect your iPad to your computer with the USB cable that came with your iPad.**

   When you connect your iPad to your computer, iTunes should start automatically. If it doesn't, chances are that you plugged the cable into a USB port on your keyboard, monitor, or hub. Try plugging it into one of the USB ports on your computer instead. Why? Because USB ports on your computer supply more power to a connected device than USB ports on a keyboard, monitor, or most hubs and the iPad requires a lot of that power — even more than an iPod or iPhone.

If iTunes still doesn't start automatically, try running it manually.

2. **Select your iPad in the iTunes sidebar.**

   You see the Welcome pane, as shown in Figure 3-1.

   If you don't see an iPad in the sidebar (at the left side of the iTunes window), and you're sure it's connected to a USB port on your computer (not the keyboard, monitor, or hub), restart your computer.

Figure 3-1: This is the first thing you see in iTunes.

3. **Click Continue.**

   iTunes presents the inevitable license agreement. After you've read the entire tome, click the I Have Read and Agree check box to select it and click Continue.

4. **Enter (or create) your Apple ID and password.**

   If you've used the iTunes Store or previously registered an Apple product, just type your Apple ID and password — otherwise, follow the directions for creating an Apple ID. After you've entered your Apple ID, click Continue.

5. **Enter your registration information.**

   After you've entered everything, click Submit to register.

6. **(Optional) Set up Find My iPad.**

   This feature helps you locate your iPad if it's lost or stolen. If you decide to use this feature, click Set Up Find My iPad to display the instructions. To skip this step, click Not Now.

7. **Name your iPad by typing a name in the Name text box.**

8. **After you click the Done button, the Summary pane should appear.**

   If the Summary pane doesn't appear, be sure your iPad is still selected on the left side of the iTunes window. Then click the Summary tab near the top of the window, as shown in Figure 3-2.

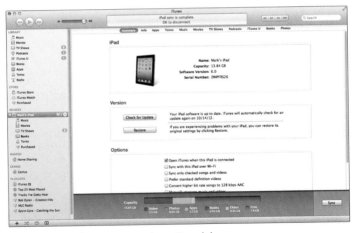

Figure 3-2: The Summary pane is pretty painless.

9. **If you want iTunes to launch automatically whenever you connect your iPad to your computer, click to put a check mark in the Open iTunes When This iPad Is Connected check box (in the Options area).**

   Why might you choose not to enable this option? If you intend to connect your iPad to your computer to charge it, for example, you might not want iTunes to launch every time you connect.

If you do choose to enable the option, iTunes will launch and synchronize automatically every time you connect your iPad.

Don't worry about this too much right now. If you change your mind, you can always come back to the Summary tab and deselect the Open iTunes When This iPad Is Connected check box.

If you do select the Open iTunes When This iPad Is Connected check box but don't want your iPad to sync automatically every time it's connected, launch iTunes and choose iTunes⟳Preferences (Mac) or Edit⟳Preferences (Windows). Click the Devices tab at the top of the window and select the Prevent iPods, iPhones, and iPads from Syncing Automatically check box. This method prevents your iPad from syncing automatically even if the Open iTunes When This iPad Is Connected option is enabled. If you choose this option, you can sync your iPad by clicking the Sync or Apply button that appears in the lower-right corner of the iTunes window when your iPad is selected in the sidebar (it says Sync in Figure 3-2).

10. **To sync automatically with your computer over a Wi-Fi connection, select the Sync with This iPad over Wi-Fi.**

    Note that enabling this option will still allow your computer to sync with your iPad when connected with the USB cable. Also, your iPad must be connected to a power source and connected to a Wi-Fi network for Wi-Fi syncing to work.

    You can also configure your iPad to allow automatic downloads of music, apps, and books that you install on other iOS 5 (and later) devices. From the Home screen, tap Settings⟳Store. Enable each of the media types that you want to automatically receive on your iPad.

11. **If you want to sync only items that have check marks to the left of their names in your iTunes library, select the Sync Only Checked Songs and Videos check box.**

12. **If you want high-definition videos you import to be automatically converted into smaller standard-definition video files when you transfer them to your iPad, select the Prefer Standard Definition Videos check box.**

Standard-definition video files are significantly smaller than high-definition video files. You'll hardly notice the difference when you watch the video on your iPad, but you'll be able to have more video files on your iPad because they take up less space.

The conversion from HD to standard definition takes a long time; be prepared for very long sync times when you sync new HD video and have this option enabled.

13. **If you want songs with bit rates higher than 128 kbps converted into smaller-size AAC files when you transfer them to your iPad, select the Convert Higher Bit Rate Songs to 128 kbps AAC check box.**

A higher bit rate means that the song will have better sound quality but use a lot of storage space. Songs that you buy at the iTunes Store or on Amazon.com, for example, have bit rates of around 256 kbps. So, a 4-minute song with a 256-kbps bit rate is around 8MB; convert it to 128-kbps AAC and it will be roughly half that size (that is, around 4MB), while sounding almost as good. Click the drop-down list to choose the target bit rate — the default is 128 kbps.

Most people won't notice much (if any) difference in audio quality when listening to music on most consumer audio gear. So unless you have your iPad hooked up to a great amplifier and superb speakers or headphones, you probably won't hear much difference. But your iPad can hold roughly twice as much music if you enable this option.

14. **If you want to turn off automatic syncing in the Music and Video panes, select the Manually Manage Music and Videos check box.**

15. **If you want to password-protect your backups (your iPad creates a backup of its contents automatically every time you sync using the cable), select the Encrypt iPad Backup check box.**

If you do decide to encrypt your backups, click the Change Password button to enter your own password.

You can also set your iPad to back up wirelessly using the iCloud Backup feature on your iPad — if you turn iCloud Backup on, iTunes will not back up your iPad data when it's connected by cable. To set things in motion, from the Home screen, tap Settings⤳iCloud⤳Storage & Backup. Swipe the iCloud Backup switch to turn it on. You can always start an iCloud Backup by tapping the Back Up Now button on this screen. (Remember, however, that your iPad must be plugged in to a power source and must be connected to a Wi-Fi network for an iCloud Backup.)

If you decide to select the Prevent iPods, iPhones, and iPads from Syncing Automatically check box on iTunes Preferences' Devices tab, you can still synchronize manually by clicking the Sync button in the lower-right corner of the window. If you've changed any sync settings since the last time you synchronized, the Sync button instead says Apply.

Disconnecting the iPad

When the iPad is syncing with your computer over a cable connection, iTunes displays a message that says that it's syncing with your iPad. After the sync is finished, iTunes displays a message that the iPad sync is complete and that it's okay to disconnect your iPad.

If you disconnect your iPad before a sync is completed, all or part of the sync may fail.

To cancel a sync so that you can *safely* disconnect your iPad, click the Cancel button at the top of the iTunes window (the one with the X icon) during the sync.

Synchronizing Your Data

Did you choose to set up data synchronization manually? If you did, your next order of business is to tell iTunes what data you want to synchronize between your iPad and your computer. You do this by selecting your iPad in the sidebar on the left side of the iTunes screen and clicking the Info tab, which is to the right of the Summary tab.

The Info pane has five sections: Contacts, Calendars, Mail Accounts, Other, and Advanced. If you're going to use iCloud, you can safely ignore the information in the Advanced section of the Info pane, which deals with replacing specified information on your iPad during a single synchronization. The following sections look at iCloud and each section except for the Advanced section.

iCloud

iCloud is Apple's free service for keeping your iPad, iPod touch, iPhone, Macs, and PCs synchronized. The big allure of iCloud is that it can "push" information, such as e-mail, calendars, contacts, and bookmarks, from your computer to and from your iPad. This pushing of data keeps those items synchronized on your iPad and computer(s) wirelessly and without human intervention. Plus, iCloud enables you to re-download apps, music, and video that you've bought from the iTunes Store and App Store at any time.

Contacts

The Contacts section of the Info pane determines how iTunes handles synchronization for your contacts. One method is to synchronize all your contacts, as shown in Figure 3-3. Or, you can synchronize any or all groups of contacts you've created in your computer's address book program. Just select the appropriate check boxes in the Selected Groups list, and only those groups will be synchronized.

Note that the section is named Sync Contacts because Figure 3-3 was captured in iTunes on a Mac, and the OS X Contacts application is what it syncs with. If you use a PC, you see a drop-down menu that gives you the choice of Outlook, Google Contacts, Windows Address Book, or Yahoo! Address Book. Don't worry — the process works the same on either platform.

The iPad syncs with the following address book programs:

- **Mac:** OS X Contacts, Yahoo! Address Book, and Google Contacts
- **PC:** Outlook, Google Contacts, Windows Address Book, or Yahoo! Address Book

Figure 3-3: This is where you set things up to synchronize your contacts.

If you use Yahoo! Address Book, select the Sync Yahoo! Address Book Contacts check box and then click the Configure button to enter your Yahoo! ID and password. If you use Google Contacts, select the Sync Google Contacts check box and then click the Configure button to enter your Google ID and password.

Syncing will never delete a contact from your Yahoo! Address Book if it has a Yahoo! Messenger ID, even if you delete that contact on the iPad or on your computer.

To delete a contact that has a Yahoo! Messenger ID, log on to your Yahoo! account with a web browser and delete the contact in your Yahoo! Address Book.

If you sync with your employer's Microsoft Exchange calendar and contacts, any personal contacts or calendars already on your iPad will be wiped out.

Calendars

The Calendars section of the Info pane determines how synchronization is handled for your appointments and events. You can synchronize all your calendars, as shown in Figure 3-4. Or you can synchronize any or all individual calendars you've created in your computer's calendar program. Just select the appropriate check boxes.

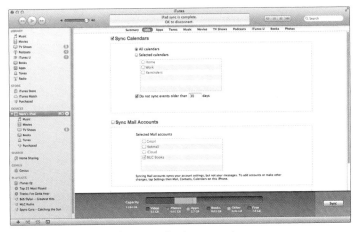

Figure 3-4: Set up sync for your calendar events here.

The Calendars section is named Sync Calendars because Figure 3-4 was captured in iTunes for the Mac. If you use a PC, this section will be named Sync Calendars with Outlook. As before, don't worry — regardless of its name, it works the same on either platform.

The iPad syncs with the following calendar programs:

✓ **Mac:** OS X Calendar

✓ **PC:** Microsoft Outlook 2003, 2007, or 2010

Mail accounts

You can sync account settings for your e-mail accounts in the Mail Accounts section of the Info pane. You can synchronize all your e-mail accounts (if you have more than one), or you can synchronize individual accounts, as shown in Figure 3-5. Just select the appropriate check boxes.

The iPad syncs with the following mail programs:

✓ **Mac:** OS X Mail

✓ **PC:** Microsoft Outlook 2003, 2007, or 2010

Figure 3-5: Transfer e-mail account settings to your iPad here.

E-mail account settings are synchronized only one way: from your computer to your iPad. If you make changes to any e-mail account settings on your iPad, the changes will *not* be synchronized back to the e-mail account on your computer. Trust us, this is a very good feature and we're glad Apple did it this way.

By the way, the password for your e-mail account may or may not be saved on your computer. If you sync an e-mail account and the iPad asks for a password when you send or receive mail, do this: From the Home screen, tap Settings⊃Mail, Contacts, Calendars. Then tap your e-mail account's name, tap Account, and then type your password in the appropriate field.

Other

The contents of the Other section depend on whether you're syncing wirelessly and with iCloud. (In other words, don't panic if the Sync Bookmarks check box doesn't appear in the Other section.) Select the check box for Sync Bookmarks if you want to sync your Safari bookmarks; don't select it if you don't care about syncing them.

Just so you know, the iPad syncs bookmarks with the following web browsers:

✔ **Mac:** Safari

✔ **PC:** Microsoft Internet Explorer and Safari

Synchronizing Your Media

If you chose to let iTunes manage synchronizing your data automatically — either by cable or wirelessly — welcome! This section looks at how you get your media — your music, podcasts, video, photos, and more — from your computer to your iPad.

Podcasts and video (but not photos) are synced only one way: from your computer to your iPad. Deleting any of these items from your iPad does not delete it from your computer when you sync. The exceptions are songs, podcasts, video, iBooks, and apps that you purchase or download using the iTunes, App Store, or iBooks apps on your iPad; and playlists you create on your iPad. Such items are, as you'd expect, copied back to your computer automatically when you sync. (You can also re-download digital media to your iPad that you've bought through the iTunes Store at any time — iCloud keeps track of everything you've purchased.) If you take photos or video using your iPad's camera — or if you save pictures from e-mail messages and web pages (by pressing and holding on an image and then tapping the Save Image button) or screen shots (which can be created by pressing the Home and Sleep/Wake buttons simultaneously) — these too can be synced.

You use the Apps, Ringtones, Music, Movies, TV Shows, Podcasts, iTunes U, Books, and Photos panes to specify the media you want to copy from your computer to your iPad. (Note that some panes won't appear unless you've added that type of media to your library — for example, iTunes U doesn't appear unless you've added something from iTunes U to your iTunes library.) The following sections explain the options you find on each pane.

To view any of these panes, make sure that your iPad is still selected in the sidebar and then click the appropriate tab near the top of the window.

The last step in each section is "Click the Sync or Apply button in the lower-right corner of the window." You have to apply changes when enabling an item for the first time, and if you make any changes to the item after that.

Apps

If you've downloaded or purchased any iPad apps from the iTunes App Store, set your automatic syncing options as follows:

1. **Click the Apps tab, and then select the Sync Apps check box.**

2. **Choose the individual apps you want to transfer to your iPad by selecting their check boxes.**

   For your convenience, you can sort your applications by name, category, size, kind, or date acquired. Or, you can type a word or phrase into the search field (the oval with the magnifying glass to the right of the words *Sync Apps*) to search for a specific app.

3. **(Optional) Rearrange app icons in iTunes by dragging them where you want them to appear on your iPad, as shown in Figure 3-6.**

4. **Click the Sync or Apply button in the lower-right corner of the window.**

   Your apps are synced and your icons are rearranged on your iPad just the way you arranged them in iTunes.

Icon being dragged to Screen 1

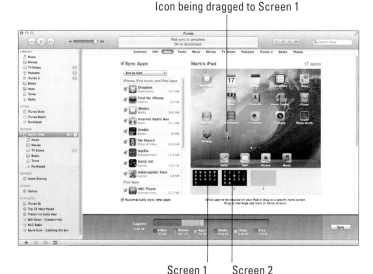

Screen 1   Screen 2

Figure 3-6: We're dragging an app icon from Home screen 2 to Home screen 1 to make it easier to get to.

Ringtones

To transfer ringtones to your iPad for use with Phone, FaceTime, and Messages, follow these steps:

1. **Click the Tones tab and select the Sync Tones check box in the Tones pane.**

2. **Choose to sync all ringtones or selected ringtones from your iTunes library.**

   Note that the Selected Tones option is disabled if you don't have any ringtones in your iTunes library.

3. **If you choose Selected Tones, include them by selecting the appropriate check boxes.**

4. **Click the Sync or Apply button in the lower-right corner of the window.**

   Your ringtones are synced.

Music, music videos, and voice memos

To transfer music to your iPad, follow these steps:

1. **Click the Music tab, and then select the Sync Music check box in the Music pane.**

2. **Select the button for Entire Music Library or Selected Playlists, Artists, Albums, and Genres.**

   If you choose the latter, select the check boxes next to particular playlists, artists, albums, and genres you want to transfer. You can also choose to include music videos, voice memos, or both by selecting the appropriate check boxes at the top of the pane (see Figure 3-7).

   If you select the Automatically Fill Free Space with Songs check box, iTunes fills any free space on your iPad with music.

3. **Click the Sync or Apply button in the lower-right corner of the window.**

   Your music, music videos, and voice memos are synced.

Figure 3-7: Use the Music pane to copy music, music videos, and voice notes from your computer to your iPad.

 Music, podcasts, and video are notorious for chewing up massive amounts of storage space on your iPad. If you try to sync too much media, you see error messages that warn you there's not enough room on your iPad for everything you tried to sync. To avoid these errors, select playlists, artists, and/or genres that total less than the free space on your iPad. To find out how much free space your iPad has, look near the bottom of the iTunes window while your iPad is selected. You see a chart that shows the contents of your iPad, color-coded for your convenience.

Movies

To transfer movies to your iPad, follow these steps:

1. **Click the Movies tab and select the Sync Movies check box.**

2. **Choose an option for movies that you want to include automatically from the pop-up menu, as shown in Figure 3-8, or select the check box for each movie you want to sync.**

 Regardless of the choices you make in the pop-up menu, you can always select individual movies by selecting their check boxes.

3. **If you also want to include movies within playlists, select the appropriate check boxes in the Include Movies from Playlists sections of the TV Shows pane.**

   Note that the Include Movies from Playlists section will not appear if you don't have any playlists that contain TV episodes.

4. **Click the Sync or Apply button in the lower-right corner of the window.**

   Your movies are synced.

Figure 3-8: Your choices in the Movies pane determine which movies are copied to your iPad.

TV shows

The procedure for syncing TV shows is slightly different than the procedure for syncing movies:

1. **Click the TV Shows tab and select the Sync TV Shows check box to enable TV show syncing.**

2. **Choose how many episodes to include from the Automatically Include pop-up menu on the left, as shown in Figure 3-9.**

3. **On the right, choose whether you want all shows or only selected shows.**

4. **If you want to also include individual episodes or episodes on playlists, select the appropriate check boxes in the Episodes and Include Episodes from Playlists sections of the TV Shows pane.**

   Note that the Include Episodes from Playlists section will not appear if you don't have any playlists that contain TV episodes.

5. **Click the Sync or Apply button in the lower-right corner of the window.**

   Your TV shows are synced.

Figure 3-9: These menus determine how TV shows are synced with your iPad.

Regardless of the choices you make in the pop-up menus, you can always select individual episodes by selecting their check boxes.

Podcasts

To transfer podcasts to your iPad, follow these steps:

1. **Click the Podcasts tab and select the Sync Podcasts check box in the Podcasts pane.**

   Two pop-up menus enable you to specify which episodes and which podcasts you want to sync (see Figure 3-10).

2. **Select how many episodes of a podcast you want to sync in the pop-up menu on the left.**

3. **Choose whether to sync all podcasts or just selected podcasts from the pop-up menu in the upper-right corner.**

4. **If you have podcast episodes on playlists, you can include them by selecting the appropriate check box under Include Episodes from Playlists.**

   Note that the Include Episodes from Playlists section will not appear if you don't have any playlists that contain podcast episodes.

5. **Click the Sync or Apply button in the lower-right corner of the window.**

   Your podcasts are synced.

Regardless of the choices you make in the pop-up menus, you can always select individual episodes by selecting their check boxes.

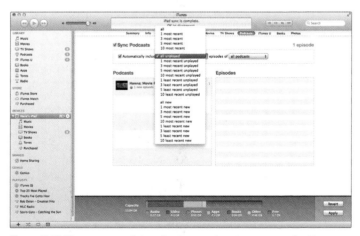

Figure 3-10: These menus determine how podcasts are synced with your iPad.

iTunes U

To sync educational content from iTunes U, follow these steps:

1. **Click the iTunes U tab and select the Sync iTunes U check box to enable iTunes U syncing.**

2. **Choose how many episodes to include.**

3. **Choose whether you want all collections or only selected collections from the two pop-up menus.**

4. **If you want to also include individual episodes or episodes on playlists, select the appropriate check boxes in the iTunes U Collections and Items sections of the iTunes U pane.**

5. **Click the Sync or Apply button in the lower-right corner of the window.**

   Your iTunes U episodes are synced.

 Regardless of the choices you make in the pop-up menus, you can always select individual episodes by selecting their check boxes.

Books

To sync iBooks and audiobooks, follow these steps:

1. **Click the Books tab and select the Sync Books check box to enable book syncing.**

2. **Choose All Books or Selected Books.**

3. **If you chose Selected Books, select the check boxes of the books you wish to sync.**

4. **Scroll down the page a little and select the Sync Audiobooks check box to enable audiobook syncing.**

5. **Choose All Audiobooks or Selected Audiobooks.**

6. **If you chose Selected Audiobooks, select the check boxes of the audiobooks you want to sync.**

If the book is divided into parts, you can select check boxes for the individual parts if you want.

7. **Click the Sync or Apply button in the lower-right corner of the window.**

Your books and audiobooks are synced.

Photos

The iPad syncs photos with the following programs:

- ✔ **Mac:** iPhoto or Aperture
- ✔ **PC:** Adobe Photoshop Album or Adobe Photoshop Elements

You can also sync photos with any folder on your computer that contains images. To sync photos, follow these steps:

1. **Click the Photos tab and select the Sync Photos From check box.**

2. **Choose an application or folder from the pop-up menu (which says iPhoto in Figure 3-11).**

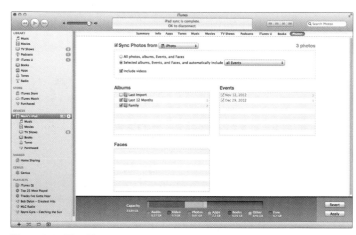

Figure 3-11: The Photos pane determines which photos will be synchronized with your iPad.

3. **To further refine what photos are synced, you may have any of the following options:**

   - *Selected albums, events, and more:* If you choose an application that supports photo albums, events, and/or facial recognition, as we have in Figure 3-11 by choosing iPhoto, you can automatically include events by making a selection from the pop-up menu or select specific albums, events, and/or faces to sync by selecting them in the following areas.

   - *Search for photos to sync:* If you're using iPhoto, you can also type a word or phrase into the search field at the top of the iTunes window (the oval with the magnifying glass) to search for a specific event or events.

   - *Select a folder of images:* If you choose a folder full of images, you can create subfolders inside it that will appear as albums on your iPad.

   But if you choose an application that doesn't support albums or events, or a single folder full of images with no subfolders, you have to transfer all or nothing.

   Because we selected iPhoto in the Sync Photos From menu, and iPhoto supports events and faces in addition to albums, we also have the option of syncing events, albums, faces, or all three.

4. **Click the Sync or Apply button in the lower-right corner of the window.**

   Your photos are synced.

Using the Notification Center

With the arrival of iOS 5, Apple introduced the *Notification Center*, which creates a single spot where you can view all notifications from your iPad apps. Instead of the constant barrage of notification messages displayed by earlier versions of iOS (from games, Mail, Calendar and a host of other apps trying to grab your attention), the Notification Center gathers everything together, and enables you to select which apps can demand your attention. Order from chaos; always *a good thing.*

To display the Notification Center, swipe downward from the top of any screen. The Center appears in Figure 3-12 — note how multiple notifications are grouped together according to the app that issued them. To open the corresponding item within the app, just tap the desired notification (for example, tapping the notification from the Calendar app opens the corresponding event within Calendar). To close the Notification Center, drag the handle at the bottom (the series of three horizontal lines) up toward the top of the screen.

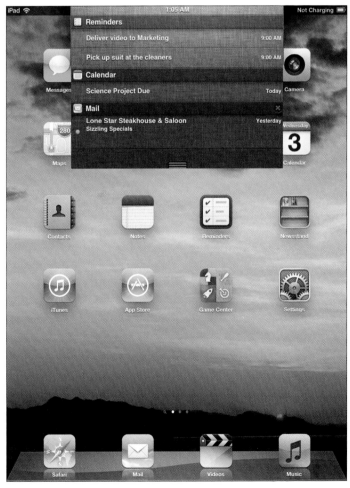

Figure 3-12: The Notification Center puts all the notification messages from your apps in one list.

Naturally, notifications will still appear on your screen as they always have — but with iOS 5 (or later) the banner messages automatically disappear after a short time (and banner text always appears at the top of the screen).

If you still find notifications disruptive (and you'd rather do without the distractions), then rejoice: iOS 5 (or later) makes it easy to minimize or eliminate them entirely. Tap the Settings icon on the Home screen and then tap the Notifications item in the list at the left side of the screen. Each app that can generate notifications appears in the list on the right. Tap the offending app, and you can remove it from the Notification Center entirely. You can also determine the type of alert that app will display (choose Alerts type if you want the old-style dialog that appears in the middle of the screen, the Banners type if you want the message to automatically disappear, or choose None to turn off notifications from that app entirely). To turn off the red badges that appear on the app, disable the Badge App Icon switch. You can also specify whether the app can display messages on your iPad's lock screen.

Chapter 4

Surfing and Sending: Web and Messaging

. . . .

In This Chapter

▷ Surfing the Net

▷ Opening and displaying web pages

▷ Using Reminders

▷ Using links, bookmarks, and history lists

▷ Getting e-mail set up

▷ Sending, reading, and managing e-mail

▷ Sending iMessages

. . . .

*T*he iPad's glorious Retina display, in combination with the powerful Apple-designed dual-core chip inside the machine, makes browsing on Apple's tablet an absolute delight.

In this chapter, you discover the pleasures — and the few roadblocks — in navigating cyberspace on your iPad.

Surfin' Dude

A version of the Apple Safari web browser is a major reason that the Net on the iPad is very much like the Net you've come to expect on a more traditional computer. Come to think of it, the Net often looks a lot better on the iPad thanks to its beautiful screen. Safari for the Mac and for Windows is one of the very best web browsers in the business.

Exploring the browser

We start your cyberexpedition with a quick tour of the Safari browser. Take a gander at Figure 4-1: Not all browser controls found on a PC or Mac are present. Still, Safari on the iPad has a familiar look and feel. We describe these controls and others throughout this chapter.

Previous

Next page

Bookmarks   Address field   Search

Add Bookmarks, reading list,
Home screen; e-mail a link;
tweet; or print

Figure 4-1: The iPad's Safari browser.

Blasting off into cyberspace

Surfing the web begins with a web address, of course. When you start by tapping the address field in iPad's Safari, the virtual keyboard appears. Here are a few tips for using the keyboard in Safari:

⮕ Because so many web addresses end with the suffix `.com` (pronounced *dot com*), the virtual keyboard has a dedicated .com key. For other common web suffixes — `.edu`, `.net`, and `.org` — press and hold the .com key and choose the relevant domain type.

⮕ Both the period (.) and the slash (/) are on the virtual keyboard because you frequently use them when entering web addresses.

⮕ The moment you tap a single letter, you see a list of web addresses that match those letters. For example, if you tap the letter *M* (see Figure 4-2), you see web listings for MSNBC, MLB, and others.

The iPad has three ways to determine websites to suggest when you tap certain letters:

⮕ **Bookmarks:** One method is the websites you already bookmarked from the Safari or Internet Explorer browsers on your computer (and synchronized, as we describe in Chapter 3).

⮕ **iCloud Tabs:** iCloud syncs the tabs you've opened on your Mac or other iOS devices, and can display them in the list of websites. (More on iCloud Tabs later in the chapter.)

⮕ **History:** The second method iPad uses when you tap a particular letter is to suggest sites from the History list — those cyberdestinations where you recently hung your hat.

You might as well open your first web page now — and it's a full *HTML* page, to borrow from techie lingo:

1. Tap the Safari icon docked at the bottom of the Home screen.

Figure 4-2: Web pages that match your search letter.

It's another member of the Fantastic Four (along with Mail, Videos, and Music). Chapter 1 introduces the Home screen.

2. **Tap the address field (refer to Figure 4-1).**

3. **Begin typing the web address on the virtual keyboard that slides up from the bottom of the screen.**

4. **Do one of the following:**

   a. To accept one of the bookmarked (or other) sites that show up on the list, merely tap the name. Safari automatically fills in the address field and takes you where you want to go.

   b. Keep tapping the proper keyboard characters until you enter the complete web address for the site you have in mind. Next, tap the Go key found on the right side of the keyboard.

It's not necessary to type **www** at the beginning of a web address. So, if you want to visit www. theonion.com (for example), typing **theonion. com** is sufficient to transport you to the humor site. For that matter, it even works if you type **theonion** without the .com.

I Can See Clearly Now

If you know how to open a web page (if you don't, read the preceding section in this chapter), we can show you how radically simple it is to zoom in on the pages so that you can read what you want to read and see what you want to see without enlisting a magnifying glass.

Try these neat tricks:

- **Double-tap the screen so that portion of the text fills the entire screen.** It takes just a second before the screen comes into focus. By way of example, check out Figure 4-3. It shows two views of the same *Sports Illustrated* web page: when you first open it and after you double-tap it. The area of the screen you double-tapped is the area that swells up. To return to the first view, double-tap the screen again.

- **Pinch the page.** Sliding your thumb and index finger together and then spreading them also zooms in and out of a page. Again, wait just a moment for the screen to come into focus.

- **Press down on a page and drag it in all directions, or flick through a page from top to bottom.** You're panning and scrolling, baby.

- **Rotate the iPad to its side.** Watch what happens to the White House website, shown in Figure 4-4. It reorients from portrait to a widescreen landscape view. The keyboard is also wider, making it a little easier to enter a new web address. This little magic won't happen if you set the Screen Rotation Lock described in Chapter 1.

Figure 4-3: Doing a double-tap dance zooms in and out.

Figure 4-4: Going wide.

When you surf the web on a computer, you rarely go to a single web page and call it a day. In fact, you likely have multiple web pages open at the same time. Sometimes, it's because you choose to hop around the web without closing the pages you visit. Sometimes, a link (see the next section) automatically opens a new page without shutting the old one. Safari on the iPad lets you view multiple web pages simultaneously using tabs — by tapping a tab at the top of the screen, it's easy to switch immediately between pages. After you have one page open, here's how to open additional web pages in Safari:

1. **Tap the New Tab icon (refer to Figure 4-1) on the left side of the navigation bar at the top of the screen.**

   The New Tab button sports a plus sign. Safari displays a new Untitled tab at the top of the page, as shown in Figure 4-5.

Figure 4-5: A second tab, all open for business.

2. Tap the address field and type a web address for your new page.

To close the tab you're currently viewing, tap the X that appears at the left side of the tab.

Looking at lovable links

Surfing the web would be a real drag if you had to enter a web address every time you want to navigate from one page to another. That's why bookmarks are so useful. And, it's why handy links are welcome, too.

Text links that transport you from one site to another are typically underlined or shown in bold type or merely items in a list. Tap the link to go directly to that site or page.

Tapping other links leads to different outcomes:

- **Open a map:** Tapping a map launches the Maps app — yep, the same one you'll find on your iPad's Home screen in Chapter 1 — and displays the map specified by the web page.

- **Prepare an e-mail:** Tap an e-mail address, and the iPad opens the Mail app (find out more about e-mailing later in this chapter) and automatically fills in the To field with that address. The virtual keyboard is also summoned so that you can add other e-mail addresses and compose a subject line and message. This shortcut doesn't work in all instances in which an e-mail appears on the web.

To see the web address where a link will send you, press your finger against the link and keep it there. (Safari also allows you to open the link in a new tab or add it to your Reading list, which we'll discuss in a page or two.) You can also use this method to determine whether a picture has a link.

The web is crawling (pun intended) with a huge array of conflicting programming and browser standards, so not every web link cooperates with the iPad. As of this writing, the iPad didn't support some common web standards — most notably,

Adobe Flash video. At press time, for example, you couldn't play videos on the iPad from the popular Hulu.com video site, among many others. But all is not lost, even with the absence of Flash. Apple does support an emerging standard for streaming audio and video called *HTML5,* as well as *HTTP.* In the meantime, if you see an incompatible link, nothing may happen — or a message may be displayed about having to install a plug-in.

Book (mark) 'em, Dano

You already know how useful bookmarks are and how you can synchronize bookmarks from the browsers on your computer (or via iCloud). It's equally simple to bookmark a web page directly on the iPad:

1. **Make sure that the page you want to bookmark is open, and tap the Action symbol at the top of the screen (which sports an arrow leaping from within a box).**

   You have the opportunity to tap Bookmark, Add to Reading List, Add to Home Screen, Mail, Facebook, Tweet, Copy, or Print. Figure 4-6 shows these options near the top of the screen.

2. **Tap the Add Bookmark option.**

   A new window opens with a default name for the bookmark, its web address, and its folder location.

3. **To accept the default bookmark name and default bookmark folder, tap Save.**

4. **To change the default bookmark name, tap the X in the circle next to the name, enter the new title (using the virtual keyboard), and then tap Save.**

5. **To change the location where the bookmark is saved, tap the > symbol in the Bookmarks field, tap the folder where you want the bookmark to be kept, tap the Add Bookmark button in the upper-left corner of the screen, and then tap Save.**

Figure 4-6: Turning into a bookie.

If you tap the > symbol, you can also choose to add the bookmark to your Bookmarks Bar, which is displayed directly under the Safari toolbar. (Note, however, that you must turn on the Bookmarks Bar in Settings. Tap Safari and tap Always Show Bookmarks Bar to display the Bar at all times.) A single tap on a bookmark on the Bar takes you right to that page. Outstanding!

To open a bookmarked page after you set it up, tap the Bookmarks icon in the upper-left portion of the screen (refer to Figure 4-1) and then tap the appropriate bookmark.

If the bookmark you have in mind is buried inside a folder, tap the folder name first and then tap the bookmark you want.

Using the Reading List

iOS 5 introduced the Safari Reading List, which enables you to save interesting pages you encounter during a surfing session for later reading. Tap the Action icon at the top of the Safari window — it's the square with the arrow at the left of the address field — and tap Add to Reading List. You can do this as often as you like while surfing.

You'll note that you can also send a Tweet with this page by tapping the Twitter button, or include this page in a Facebook post by tapping the Facebook button.

To display the Reading List, tap the Bookmarks icon at the top of the window (it looks like an open book) and tap the Reading List icon (which looks like a pair of eyeglasses). Tap a story to view the page, and the story is automatically removed from the list. With the arrival of iOS 6, you don't need an active Internet connection to view the pages that you've saved. The Reading List now works the same when you're offline and out of the range of a Wi-Fi or cellular data connection.

Keeping tabs through iCloud

With iCloud Tabs, you can visit a web page that you've opened recently on any other iOS 6 device, or on your Mac (running OS X Mountain Lion 10.8 or later). Unlike bookmarks, these web pages are constantly updated automatically as you use devices (much like a shared History list). Tap the iCloud Tabs button at the top of the screen, and you'll see a list of pages (synced via iCloud) that you've recently opened on your Mac or other iOS 6 devices. Each page in the list is sorted by the device or computer that opened them. Tap the page to load it on your iPad.

You must be using the same Apple ID on all your computers and devices for iCloud Tabs to work. If no other devices are using the same Apple ID, the iCloud Tabs icon doesn't appear at the top of your Safari screen.

Putting Reminders to Work

It's time to banish that old appointment book (or even worse, that stack of tiny scraps of paper in your wallet or purse). With Reminders, your iPad can hold your to-do list (and keep it updated automatically across all your iOS devices using iCloud). Reminders works with OS X Calendar and Outlook too, keeping track of events between your computer and your iPad.

To get started, tap the Reminders icon on the Home screen. You'll see the layout shown in Figure 4-7. To add a new reminder for a specific day, tap the day on the calendar to highlight it and then tap the Add icon (which carries a plus sign) at the top-right corner of the screen. The virtual keyboard appears, enabling you to type the text of your reminder. When you're finished, tap the Hide Keyboard button at the lower-right corner. Now you can tap the item itself, which displays the Details dialog; from here, you can set a reminder and specify whether this is a repeating event.

After you've taken care of a to-do item, you can tap the check box next to it to indicate that it's been completed. To delete a reminder, display the Details dialog again and tap Delete.

To search for a specific reminder, tap in the Search Reminders box (next to the magnifying glass) and type the text you want to match.

Figure 4-7: The Reminders screen.

Setting Up Your E-Mail

To use Mail, you need an e-mail address. If you have broadband Internet access (that is, a cable modem, FIOS, or DSL), you probably received one or more e-mail addresses when you signed up. If you're one of the handful of readers who doesn't already have an e-mail account, you can get one for free from Yahoo! (http://mail.yahoo.com), Google (http://mail.google.com), AOL (www.aol.com/), Microsoft (www.hotmail.com), or numerous other service providers.

Set up your account the easy way

Chapter 3 explains the option of automatically syncing the
e-mail accounts on your Windows PC or Mac with your iPad.
If you chose that option, your e-mail accounts should be configured on your iPad already. You may proceed directly to the
later section "Darling, You Send Me."

If you haven't yet chosen that option but want to set up your
account the easy way now, go to Chapter 3 and read that section, sync your iPad, and then you, too, can proceed directly
to the section "Darling, You Send Me," later in this chapter.

Set up your account the less easy way

If you don't want to sync the e-mail accounts on your computer, you can set up an e-mail account on your iPad manually. It's not quite as easy as clicking a box and syncing your
iPad, but it's not rocket science, either.

If you have no e-mail accounts on your iPad, the first time
you launch Mail you'll be walked through the following procedure. If you have one or more e-mail accounts on your
iPad already and want to add a new account manually, from
the Home screen, start by tapping Settings⇨Mail, Contacts,
Calendars⇨Add Account.

You should now be staring at the Add Account screen.
Proceed to one of the next two sections, depending on your
e-mail account.

Setting up an e-mail account with Microsoft Exchange, Yahoo! Mail, Google, AOL, or Hotmail

If your account is with Yahoo!, Google (Gmail), AOL, your
company's Microsoft Exchange server, or Microsoft's Hotmail
service, tap the appropriate button on the Add Account
screen now. If your account is with a provider other than
these five, tap the Other button and skip ahead to the next
section.

Enter your name, e-mail address, and password. There's a field for a description of this account (such as work or personal), but it tends to fill in automatically with the same contents in the Address field unless you tell it differently.

Tap the Next button in the top-right corner of the screen, and you can specify whether contacts, calendars, and reminders from this account should be included on your iPad. After you've made your choices and tapped Save, you're finished. That's all there is to setting up your account.

Setting up an account with another provider

If your e-mail account is with a provider other than Yahoo!, Google, AOL, or Microsoft, you have a bit more work ahead of you. You're going to need a bunch of information about your e-mail account that you may not know or have handy.

We suggest that you scan the following instructions, note the items you don't know, and go find the answers before you continue. To find the answers, look at the documentation you received when you signed up for your e-mail account, or visit the account provider's website and search there. If you're planning to use your company e-mail account, your company's network administrator can supply you with the information you need.

Here's how you set up an account:

1. **On the Add Account screen, tap the Other button.**

2. **Under Mail, tap Add Mail Account; fill in the name, address, password, and description in the appropriate fields.**

3. **Tap Next.**

   With any luck, that's all you'll have to do. The iPad will look up and retrieve your account credentials. Otherwise, continue with Step 4.

4. **Tap the button at the top of the screen that denotes the type of e-mail server this account uses: IMAP or POP.**

5. **Fill in the Internet host name for your incoming mail server, which should look something like** `mail.providername.com`.

6. **Fill in your username and password.**

7. **Enter the Internet host name for your outgoing mail server, which should look something like** `smtp.providername.com`.

8. **Enter your username and password in the appropriate fields.**

9. **Tap the Next button in the upper-right corner to create the account.**

Some outgoing mail servers don't need your username and password. The fields for these items on your iPad note that they're optional. Still, we suggest that you fill them in anyway. It saves you from having to add them later if your outgoing mail server *does* require an account name and password, which many do these days.

Darling, You Send Me

Now that your account or accounts are set up, we look at how to use your iPad to send e-mail. You see several subspecies of messages: pure text, text with a photo, a partially finished message (a *draft*) that you want to save and complete later, a reply to an incoming message, and forwarding an incoming message to someone else, for example. The following sections examine these subsets one at a time. You also find a final section that explains handy settings for sending e-mail messages.

Sending an all-text message

To compose a new e-mail message, tap Mail on the Home screen. What you see next depends on how you're holding your iPad. In landscape mode (see Figure 4-8), your e-mail accounts or e-mail folders are listed in a panel along the left side of the screen, with the actual message filling the larger panel on the right.

Reply, forward, or print

Delete ——— Compose
new
Move ——— message

Flag

Figure 4-8: When holding the iPad sideways, Mail looks like this.

Depending on the last time the mail application was open, you may instead see message previews in the left panel when your iPad is horizontal. Message previews show the name of the sender, the subject header, and the first two lines of the message. (In Settings, you can change the number of lines shown in the preview — anywhere from one line to five lines. Or, you can show no preview lines.)

When you hold the iPad in portrait mode, the last incoming message fills the entire screen. Figure 4-9 shows this view. You have to tap an Inbox button (in the upper-left corner of the screen) to summon a panel that shows other accounts or message previews. These overlay the message that otherwise fills the screen.

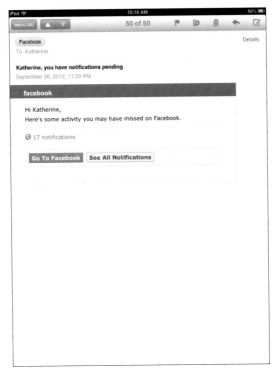

Figure 4-9: When holding the iPad in portrait mode, the message fills the screen.

Now, to create a new message, follow these steps:

1. **Tap the Compose New Message button (refer to Figure 4-8).**

   A screen like the one shown in Figure 4-10 appears.

2. **Type the names or e-mail addresses of the recipients in the To field, or tap the + button to the right of the To field to choose a contact or contacts from your iPad's contacts list.**

3. **(Optional) Tap the field labeled Cc/Bcc, From.**

   Doing so breaks them out into separate Cc, Bcc, and From fields.

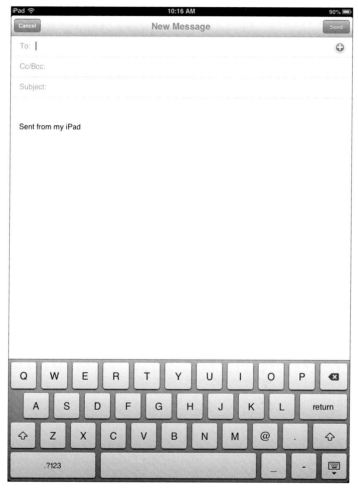

Figure 4-10: The New Message screen appears, ready for you to start typing the recipient's name.

The Cc/Bcc label stands for *carbon copy/blind carbon copy.* Carbon copy is kind of an FYI to a recipient. It's like saying, "We figure you'd appreciate knowing this, but you don't need to respond."

When using Bcc, you can include a recipient on the message, but other recipients can't see that this recipient has been included. It's great for those secret agent e-mails! Tap the respective Cc or Bcc field to type names. Or, tap the + symbol that appears in those fields to add a contact.

4. **(Optional) If you tap From, you can choose to send the message from any of your e-mail accounts on the fly, assuming, of course, that you have more than one account set up on the iPad.**

If you start typing an e-mail address, e-mail addresses that match what you typed appear in a list below the To or Cc field. If the correct one is in the list, tap it to use it.

5. **Type a subject in the Subject field.**

The subject is optional, but it's considered poor form to send an e-mail message without one.

6. **Type your message in the message area.**

The message area is immediately below the Subject field. You have ample space to get your message across.

7. **Tap the Send button in the upper-right corner of the screen.**

Your message wings its way to its recipients almost immediately. If you aren't in range of a Wi-Fi network or the AT&T EDGE or 3G/4G data network when you tap Send, the message is sent the next time you're in range of one of these networks.

Apple includes a bunch of landscape-orientation keyboards in various applications, including Mail. When you rotate the iPad to its side, you can compose a new message using a wider-format virtual keyboard.

Sending a photo with a text message

Sometimes a picture is worth a thousand words. When that's the case, here's how to send an e-mail message with a photo enclosed:

1. **Tap the Photos icon on the Home screen.**

2. **Find the photo you want to send.**

3. **Tap the Action button (which looks like a little rect-angle with a curved arrow springing out of it) in the upper-right corner of the screen.**

4. **Tap the Mail button.**

   An e-mail message appears onscreen with the photo already attached. In fact, the image appears to be embedded in the body of the message, but the recipient receives it as a regular e-mail attachment.

5. **Address the message and type whatever text you like, as you did for an all-text message in the preceding section, and then tap the Send button.**

 If you've already composed a new message and then decide to enclose a photo or video, you can double-tap within the body of the message where you'd like to insert the photo or video and then tap the Insert Photo or Video button that appears.

Replying to or forwarding an e-mail message

When you receive a message and want to reply to it, open the message and then tap the Reply/Reply All/Forward button, which looks like a curved arrow at the upper-right corner of the screen, as shown in Figure 4-11. Then tap the Reply, Reply All, or Forward button.

The Reply button creates a blank e-mail message addressed to the sender of the original message. The Reply All button creates a blank e-mail message addressed to the sender and all other recipients of the original message, plus CCs. (The Reply All option appears only if more than one recipient was on the original e-mail.) In both cases, the subject is retained with a *Re:* prefix added. So if the original subject was *iPad Tips,* the reply's subject is *Re: iPad Tips.*

Tapping the Forward button creates an unaddressed e-mail message that contains the text of the original message. Add the e-mail address(es) of the person or people you want to forward the message to, and then tap Send. In this case, rather than a *Re:* prefix, the subject is preceded by *Fwd:.* So this time, the subject is *Fwd: iPad Tips.*

Figure 4-11: Reading and managing an e-mail message.

To send your reply or forwarded message, tap the Send button as usual.

Working with Mail Messages

The first half of the mail equation is sending mail, of course. Now it's time for the second half — receiving and reading the stuff.

You can tell when you have *unread* mail by looking at the Mail icon at the bottom of your Home screen. The cumulative number of unread messages appears in a little red circle in the upper-right area of the icon.

You can also set Mail to display notifications using the new Notification Center. From the Settings screen, tap Notifications and then tap the Mail entry to choose the desired notification type.

Reading messages

To read your mail, tap the Mail icon on the Home screen. Remember that what appears on the screen depends on whether you're holding the iPad in portrait or landscape mode, and what was on the screen the last time you opened the Mail application. When held in landscape mode, you'll see All Inboxes at the top of the Inboxes section, which, as its name suggests, is a repository for all the messages across all your accounts. The number to the right of All Inboxes should match the number on the Mail icon on your Home page. Again, it's the cumulative tally of unread messages across all your accounts. (If you have only one mail account, you'll see only that account instead of All Inboxes.)

Below the All Inboxes listing are the inboxes for your individual accounts. The tally this time is only for the unread messages in those accounts. If you tap the listings here, you'll see any subfolders for each individual account (Drafts, Sent Mail, Trash, and so on). Messages are displayed in threads or conversations, making them easy to follow. Of course, you can still view accounts individually. Follow these steps to read your e-mail:

1. **If the e-mail mailbox you want to see isn't front and center, tap the Accounts button in the upper-left corner of the screen to summon the appropriate one.**

   Again, this button may say Inbox or some other folder name, or it may say the name of the e-mail account that is currently open.

2. **(Optional) Drag the top of the screen down to check for new messages.**

3. **Tap one of the inboxes or accounts to check for any new messages within those mailboxes. To summon the unified inbox, tap All Inboxes instead.**

   If a blue dot appears next to a message, it means that the message has not been read. When you open a mailbox by tapping it, the iPad displays the number of "recent" messages that you specify in Settings — 50 by default, though you can display up to 1,000. To see more than the number you specified, tap Load Additional Messages.

4. **Tap a message to read it.**

   When a message is on the screen, the buttons for managing incoming messages appear at the top of the screen, most of which you're already familiar with. If you're holding the iPad in portrait mode, you'll see up/down arrows that correspond to the next or previous message. (Refer to Figure 4-11.)

5. **In landscape mode (and from within an account), tap a preview listing to the left of a message to read the next or previous message or any other visible message on the list. Scroll up or down to find other messages to read.**

A number next to one of the previews indicates the number of related messages in a conversation or *thread.*

Under a thread, only the first message of the conversation displays in the inbox. Tap that message to reveal the entire back and forth. You can turn message threading off by tapping Settings⟹Mail, Contacts, Calendars⟹Organize By Thread.

Have you noticed the new mailbox named VIP yet? Your VIP mailbox holds incoming messages from just the folks you specify: family, friends, your company, whoever's a VIP in your book. To set up your VIP list, tap the VIP entry within the Mailbox screen, tap the Add VIP button, and select one or more contacts. VIPs are also synced through iCloud, so any VIP you add on your iPad will also be automatically added as a VIP on your iPhone (running iOS 6) and Mac (running OS X Mountain Lion 10.8 or later).

Managing messages

Managing messages typically involves either moving the messages to a folder or deleting them. To herd your messages into folders, you have the following options:

✓ **To flag a message or mark it as unread,** tap the Flag icon that appears at the top right. Then choose whether you want to flag it in the message list (Mail adds a tiny red flag icon) or mark it as unread.

✔ **To move a message in another folder,** tap the Move Message icon. When the list of folders appears, tap the folder where you want to file the message.

✔ **To move messages to another folder in bulk,** tap Edit. In both portrait and landscape, Edit appears at the top of your inbox or another mailbox when those mail folders are selected. After tapping Edit, it becomes a Cancel button and buttons labeled Delete (in red) and Move (in blue) appear at the bottom of the screen. Tap the circle to the left of each message you want to move so that a check mark appears. Tap Move and tap the new folder in which you want those messages to hang out.

✔ **To read a message that you've moved,** tap the folder where the message now resides, and tap the header or preview for the message in question.

✔ **To print a message,** tap the Reply, Forward, Print button (refer to Figure 4-11) and then tap Print.

Delete a message by tapping the Delete Message icon. You have a chance to cancel in case you tap the Delete Message icon by mistake. You can delete e-mail messages without opening them in two ways:

✔ Swipe left or right across the message in its preview pane, and then tap the red Delete button that appears to the right of the message.

✔ Tap the Edit button, and tap the little circle to the left of each message you want to remove. Tapping that circle puts a check mark in it and brightens the red Delete button at the bottom of the screen. Tap that Delete button to erase all messages you checked off. Deleted messages are moved to the Trash folder.

Doing the iMessage Thing

What if we told you that you could send unlimited text messages to anyone with a Mac (running OS X Lion or later), iPad, iPhone, or iPod touch that's running iOS 5 (or later)? Yes, it's indeed cool, but wait — what if I also told you it was *free*? (Oh, and you can send those old-fashioned SMS and MMS text messages too, but we all know how much that costs.)

Welcome to iMessage, which is built-in to your iPad's Messages app. With iMessage, you can send text, photos, video, contacts, and even your current location to another person, using either a Wi-Fi or 3G/4G cellular connection. (Remember, you can't send an SMS or MMS message over a Wi-Fi connection — only your carrier can handle that.)

The first time you run Messages, you'll enter the e-mail address that the app will use to send and receive messages. (Note that this e-mail account need not be the same account you use for your Apple ID.) When Messages has verified the address, you'll see the app's main screen.

To send a message, tap the New Message icon (the square with the pencil) at the top of the screen. You can either type the recipient's e-mail address (using the virtual keyboard shown in Figure 4-12), or tap the round icon with the plus sign to select a contact from your Contacts list. (Note that if your recipient is using an iPhone, you'll be using that person's telephone number within Messages.)

You can add multiple recipients, just as you can within Mail.

After you've added all your recipients, tap within the text box (right above the virtual keyboard) and begin typing. You can tap the camera icon next to the text box at any time to add either a photo or video from your existing library on your iPad, or you can shoot a video clip or take a photo immediately.

When you're ready to send the message, tap the Send button. You'll see your conversation take place at the right side of the window. Your message bubbles appear on the right, and your recipient's messages appear on the left (this is very familiar to any Mac owner who's used iChat or the OS X version of Messages in the past).

Messages keeps track of your conversations in the list on the left, and you can return to any conversation by tapping it. To delete a conversation, tap the Edit button, tap the red circle icon to the left of the offending conversation, and then tap Delete.

Figure 4-12: Preparing to send an iMessage.

Chapter 5
Music, Movies, and Books

In This Chapter

- Getting familiar with the iPod inside your iPad
- Playing music with the controls, Genius, and playlist features
- Finding video to watch
- Chatting with FaceTime
- Using the Camera and Photo Booth apps
- Opening up to iBooks
- Shopping the iBookstore
- Reading books and periodicals on your iPad

*Y*our iPad is perhaps the best iPod ever — especially for working with audio, photos, and video. In this chapter, we show you how to use your iPad to play music and movies, take photos, video chat with friends and family, and read books.

We assume that you already synced your iPad with your computer and your iPad contains audio content — songs, podcasts, or audiobooks. If you don't have any media on your iPad yet, we humbly suggest that you get some (flip to Chapter 3 and follow the instructions) before reading further.

Introducing the iPod inside Your iPad

To use your iPad as an iPod, just tap the Music icon on the right side of the dock at the bottom of the screen (unless you've moved it elsewhere).

Here's a quick overview of what you see when the Music app starts up:

- **Content window:** Across the majority of the screen, you'll see thumbnails representing your iPad audio library, which contains all the music, podcasts, audiobooks, and playlists you've synced with or purchased on your iPad. You can tap on any of these items.

- **Player controls:** At the top-left corner of the screen, from left to right, you can see the Rewind/Previous button, the Play/Pause button, the Fast Forward/Next button, the Scrubber bar (for quickly moving through a track), and the volume control.

- **Playlist and tab navigation:** When you're viewing your library in playlist mode, you can tap the New button to create a new playlist. At the bottom of the screen, from left to right, you can see a button for the iTunes Store, as well as five tabs: Playlists, Songs, Artists, Albums, and More. (Tap the More button to view Podcasts, Audiobooks, Genres, and Composers.)

We take a closer look at all these features, but for now, Figure 5-1 shows all of them for your enjoyment and edification.

Rewind

Volume control

Play/Pause

Scrubber/Playhead

Fast forward

Shuffle

Repeat

Genius

iTunes Store

Tabs

Search field

Playlist thumbnail

New playlist

Figure 5-1: These components are what you'll find on the Music app's main screen.

Check Out Your Library

The Songs tab in your library displays every single song on your iPad.

If you don't see every song in your library, chances are you've typed something into the Search field.

Finding music with the Search box

You can find a particular song, artist, album, genre, or composer in several ways.

With the Music app open, the easiest way to find music is to type a song, artist, album, or composer name into the Search field in the lower-right corner of the screen.

You can also find songs (or artists, for that matter) without opening the Music app by typing their names in a Spotlight search, as we mention in Chapter 2.

Browsing among the tabs

If you'd rather browse your music library, tap the appropriate tab at the bottom of the screen — Playlists, Songs, Artists, Albums, or More (and its submenus) — and the items of that type appear.

Now you can find a track by flicking upward or downward to scroll up and down the list or thumbnail display until you find what you're looking for in your library.

Here's what happens when you tap an item, based on which tab is selected:

- **Playlists:** The thumbnail expands into a list of the songs you've added to the chosen playlist. You can choose an individual song from the playlist, or just tap the Play button to begin with the first song in the playlist.
- **Songs:** The song plays.

If you aren't sure which song to listen to, try this: Tap the Shuffle button at the right side of the Scrubber bar. Your iPad then plays songs from your music library at random.

✔ **Artists:** The thumbnail expands into a list of all the albums and songs by that artist. Tap a song and it plays. To return to the thumbnail list of artists, you can either tap the Artists button at the top-left corner of the screen or tap the Artists tab at the bottom of the screen.

✔ **Albums:** Albums works pretty much the same way as artists except you see a grid of album covers instead of a list of artists. Tap an album and its contents appear in an overlay.

To play one of the songs on the album, tap it. To return to the grid of album covers, tap anywhere outside the overlay.

✔ **Genres:** When you tap the More tab and then tap Genres from the pop-up menu, a grid of genres appears. Tap a genre and a list of the songs in that genre appears in an overlay.

If the list of songs in an overlay is long, you may have to flick upward to see the rest of the songs.

✔ **Composers:** When you tap the More tab and then tap Composers from the pop-up menu, a list of composer thumbnails appears. Tap a composer and all the albums and songs by that composer appear. Tap a song and it plays. Tap the Composers button at the top-left corner of the screen or tap the Composers tab at the bottom of the screen to return to the list of composers.

✔ **Audiobooks:** When you tap the More tab and then tap Audiobooks from the pop-up menu, a list of thumbnails appears. Tap a thumbnail to see an overlay of the tracks — tap a track and it plays.

If you have no audiobooks synced to your iPad, the Audiobook menu item won't show up in the More pop-up menu.

Taking Control of Your Tunes

Now that you have the basics down and can find and play songs and audiobooks, we look at some of the things you can do with your iPad when it's in iPod mode.

Playing with the audio controls

First things first: We look at the controls you'll use after you tap a song, podcast, audiobook, or iTunes U course. We refer to all these things as *tracks* to avoid confusion (and unnecessary typing).

Take a peek at Figure 5-1 and you can see exactly where all these controls are located on the screen:

- **Rewind/Previous button:** When a track is playing, tap once to go to the beginning of the track or tap twice to go to the start of the preceding track in the list. Touch and hold this button to rewind the track at double speed.

- **Play/Pause button:** Tap to play or pause the track.

- **Fast Forward/Next button:** Touch and hold this button to fast-forward at double speed. Tap to skip to the next track in the list.

You can display playback controls anytime a track is playing. Better still, this trick works even when you're using another application or your home screen(s): Just double tap the Home button or swipe upward with four or five fingers to display the Icon tray and then swipe the tray from left to right. The controls appear at the bottom of the screen, as shown in Figure 5-2.

The playback controls *won't* appear if you're using an app that has its own audio, like many games; any app that records audio; and VoIP (Voice over IP) apps, such as Skype.

A similar set of controls appears at the *top* of the screen when you double-tap the Home button while your iPad is locked.

Figure 5-2: These controls appear when you double-press the Home button and swipe the tray while a track is playing.

✔ **Repeat:** Tap the circular dual-arrow once to repeat all songs in the current *list* (that is, playlist, album, artist, composer, or genre) and play them all over and over. Tap again to repeat the current *song* repeatedly. Tap again to turn off repeat.

The button appears in blue after one tap, in blue with a little 1 inside after two taps, and in black and white when repeat is turned off.

✔ **Scrubber bar and playhead:** Drag the little red line (the playhead) along the Scrubber bar to skip to any point within the track.

You can adjust the scrub rate by sliding your finger downward on the screen as you drag the playhead along the Scrubber bar. The farther down you slide your finger, the slower the scrub rate. Neat!

✔ **Shuffle:** Tap this button to play songs at random; tap again to play songs in the order they appear on the screen.

✔ **Genius:** This feature is so cool we devote an entire section to it. See the section "Using the Genius feature," later in this chapter.

✔ **Volume control:** Drag the little dot left or right to reduce or increase the volume level.

But wait, there's more. You can view the album art for the current track in a full-screen display — just tap the album art thumbnail in the Now Playing area at the top center of the screen. Now, tap anywhere on the artwork that fills the screen and the familiar controls appear again on the black Now Playing screen, as shown in Figure 5-3.

Earlier in this section, we explain how to use the Volume control, Rewind/Previous button, Play/Pause button, Fast Forward/Next button, and Scrubber bar/Playhead. They work in exactly the same way on the Now Playing screen.

Back   Track List

Figure 5-3: You see these additional controls after you tap the album art in the Now Playing area.

The new controls you see are as follows:

✓ **Track List:** Tap this button at the lower right of the Now Playing screen to see all the tracks on the album that contains the song currently playing, as shown in Figure 5-4.

Tap any song on this list to play it. Or swipe your finger across the dots just beneath the Scrubber bar to rate the song from one to five stars. In Figure 5-4, we've rated the song four stars.

Figure 5-4: We've given this tune four (out of five) stars.

Why would you want to assign star ratings to songs? One reason is that you can use star ratings to filter songs in iTunes on your Mac or PC. Another is that you can use them when you create Smart Playlists in iTunes.

✔ **Back:** Tap this button at the lower-left corner of the Now Playing screen to return to the previous screen.

Using the Genius feature

Genius selects songs from your music library that go great together. To use it, tap the Genius button, and your iPad generates a Genius playlist of songs that it picked because it thinks they go well with the song that's playing.

To use the Genius feature on your iPad, you need to turn on Genius in iTunes on your computer and then sync your iPad at least one time.

If you tap the Genius button on the main screen (refer to Figure 5-1) and no song is currently playing, a new Genius playlist thumbnail appears.

Tap the Genius playlist thumbnail and you'll see the songs that Genius selected. You see two new buttons appear in the upper-right corner of the list:

- **Refresh:** See a list of different songs that "go great with" the song you're listening to (or song you selected).

- **Save:** Save this Genius playlist so that you can listen to it whenever you like.

When you save a Genius playlist, it inherits the name of the song it's based upon and appears in your library with a Genius icon that looks like the Genius button. The next time you sync your iPad, the Genius playlist magically appears in iTunes.

Creating playlists

Playlists let you organize songs around a particular theme or mood: operatic arias, romantic ballads, British invasion — whatever. When you click the Playlists button at the bottom of the Music screen, your playlists appear in alphabetical order as thumbnails.

Although it may be easier to create playlists in iTunes on your computer, your iPad makes it relatively easy to create (and listen to) playlists:

- **To create a playlist on your iPad,** click the New button at the upper right (refer to Figure 5-1 for its location). Name your playlist and then tap Save. After you do this, you see a list of the songs on your iPad in alphabetical order. Tap the ones you want to have in this playlist and they turn gray. To add all songs on your iPad, click the Add All Songs button. When you've tapped every song you want in the list, tap the Done button just below the volume control.

✔ **To listen to a playlist,** tap the Playlist button at the bottom of the screen (if necessary) and then tap the desired playlist thumbnail. Tap a song in the list and the song will play. When that song is over or you tap the Next Song button, the next song in the playlist will play. This will continue until the last song in the playlist has played.

If your playlist is a Smart Playlist, you can tap Shuffle at the top of the list to hear a song from that playlist (and all subsequent songs) at random. When all songs in the playlist have been played, your iPad stops playing music.

Although you can't create Smart Playlists on your iPad, they totally rock. What is a Smart Playlist? Glad you asked. It's a special playlist that selects tracks based on criteria you specify, such as Artist Name, Date Added, Rating, Genre, Year, and many others. Fire up iTunes on your computer and choose File⟹New Smart Playlist to get started.

Finding Stuff to Watch

You can find and watch videos on your iPad in a couple of different ways. You can fetch all sorts of fare from the iTunes Store, whose virtual doors you can open directly from the iPad. You can download purchases you've already made on the iTunes Store using iCloud. Or, you can sync content that already resides on your PC or Mac. (If you haven't done so yet, read Chapter 3 for all the details.)

The videos you can watch on the iPad generally fall into one of the following categories:

✔ **Movies, TV shows, and music videos that you purchase or fetch free in the iTunes Store:** You can watch these by tapping the Videos icon on the Home screen.

The iTunes Store features dedicated sections for purchasing or renting episodes of TV shows and for buying or renting movies, as shown in Figure 5-5.

Figure 5-5: Buying and watching movies on the iPad couldn't be easier.

The typical price as of this writing is $1.99 to pick up a single episode of a popular TV show in standard definition or $2.99 for high-def versions. You can rent certain shows commercial-free for 99 cents. Or, you might purchase a complete season of a favorite show. The final season of *Lost,* for example, costs $24.99 in standard-def and $29.99 in high-def.

Feature films fetch prices from $9.99 to $19.99.

You can also rent some movies, typically for $2.99, $3.99, or $4.99. We're not wild about current rental restrictions — you have 30 days to begin watching a rented flick and a day to finish watching after you've started, though you can watch as often you want during the 24-hour period. Such films appear in their own Rented Movies section in the video list, which you get to by tapping Videos. The number of days before your rental expires is displayed. And you have to completely download a movie onto your iPad before you can start watching it.

As shown in Figure 5-6, by tapping a movie listing in iTunes, you can generally watch a trailer before buying (or renting) and check out additional tidbits: plot summary, credits, reviews, and customer ratings, as well as other movies that appealed to the buyer of this one. And you can search films by genre or top charts (the ones other people are buying or renting), or rely on the Apple Genius feature for recommendations based on stuff you've already watched.

- ✏ **The boatload of video podcasts, just about all of them free, featured in the iTunes Store:** Podcasts started out as another form of Internet radio, although instead of listening to live streams, you download files onto your computer or iPod to take in at your leisure. You can still find lots of audio podcasts, but the focus here is on video. You can watch free episodes that cover *Sesame Street* videos, sports programming, investing strategies, political shows (across the ideological spectrum), and so much more. To enjoy podcasts, download and run Apple's free Podcast app from the App Store.

- ✏ **Videos that play via entertainment apps:** For example, Netflix offers an app that enables you to use your Netflix subscription to stream video on your iPad. You can download the YouTube app, which plays videos from the popular Internet site. Similarly, both ABC and NBC television networks offer appealing apps so that you can catch up on their shows on your iPad.

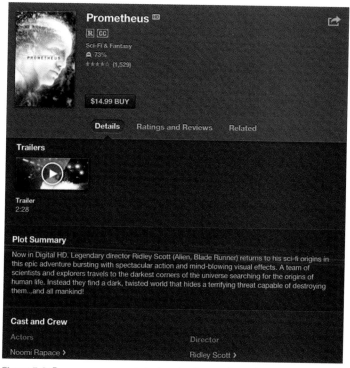

Figure 5-6: Bone up on a movie before buying or renting it.

- Seminars at Harvard, Stanford, or numerous other prestigious institutions: iTunes University boasts more than 250,000 free lectures from around the world, many of them videos. Figure 5-7 shows the iTunes U description for Open University's The Galapagos, one of the learned videos we watched. To view iTunes U content, download the free iTunes U iPad app from the App Store.

- The movies you've created in iMovie software or other software on the Mac or, for that matter, other programs on the PC: Plus all the other videos you may have downloaded from the Internet.

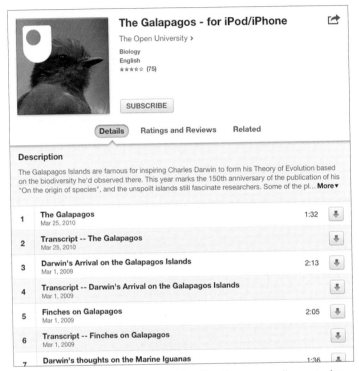

The Galapagos - for iPod/iPhone

The Open University >

Biology
English
★★★★☆ (75)

SUBSCRIBE

Details   Ratings and Reviews   Related

Description

The Galapagos Islands are famous for inspiring Charles Darwin to form his Theory of Evolution based on the biodiversity he'd observed there. This year marks the 150th anniversary of the publication of his "On the origin of species", and the unspoilt islands still fascinate researchers. Some of the pl... **More▼**

1	**The Galapagos** Mar 25, 2010	1:32
2	**Transcript -- The Galapagos** Mar 25, 2010	
3	**Darwin's Arrival on the Galapagos Islands** Mar 1, 2009	2:13
4	**Transcript -- Darwin's Arrival on the Galapagos Islands** Mar 1, 2009	
5	**Finches on Galapagos** Mar 1, 2009	2:05
6	**Transcript -- Finches on Galapagos** Mar 1, 2009	
7	Darwin's thoughts on the Marine Iguanas	1:36

Figure 5-7: Get smart. iTunes University offers lectures on diverse topics.

You may have to prepare these videos so that they'll play on your iPad. To do so, highlight the video in question after it resides in your iTunes library. Go to the Advanced menu in iTunes, and click Create iPad or Apple TV Version. Alas, this doesn't work for all the video content you download off the Internet, including video files in the AVI, DivX, MKV, and Xvid formats. You need help transferring them to iTunes and converting them to iPad-friendly formats from other software programs added to your PC or Mac.

Playing Video

Now that you know what you want to watch, here's how to watch it:

1. On the Home screen, tap the Videos icon.

Videos stored on your iPad are segregated by category — Movies, Rented Movies, TV Shows, and Music Videos. For each category, you see the program's poster art, as shown in Figure 5-8. Some categories (such as Rented Movies), appear if you have that type of content loaded on the machine.

2. **At the top of the screen, select the tab that corresponds to the type of video you want to watch.**

3. **Tap the poster that represents the movie, TV show, or other video you want to watch.**

You see a description of the video you want to watch, as shown in Figure 5-9. For a movie, the description even includes a listing of cast and filmmakers. (If you've picked a movie with chapters, tap the Chapters tab to browse the chapters. You see thumbnail images and the length of the chapter.)

Figure 5-8: Choosing a movie, TV show, or music video to watch.

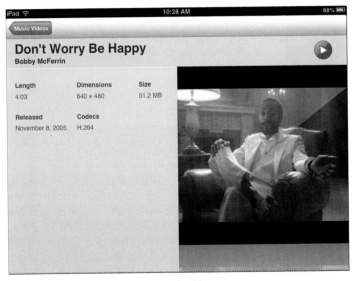

Figure 5-9: Preparing to watch a music video.

4. **To start playing a movie (or resume playing from where you left off), tap the Play arrow. Or from the Chapters view, tap any chapter to start playing from that point.**

   If you go to Settings from the Home screen and tap Video, you can change the default setting of playing from where you left off to playing from the beginning. You can also turn on Closed Captioning for those media types that support it.

5. **(Optional) Rotate your iPad to landscape mode to maximize a movie's display.**

   If you hold the iPad in portrait mode, you can see black bars on top of and below the screen where the movie is playing. Those bars remain when you rotate the device to its side, but the iPad is now playing the film in a wider-screen mode.

   For movies, this is a great thing. You can watch flicks as the filmmaker intended, in a cinematic *aspect ratio.*

By using an Apple Digital AV Adapter and an HDMI cable (or by using AirPlay with an Apple TV unit), your iPad can display the same video on both the built-in screen and a TV with an

HDMI port. (Only the very first iPad model doesn't have this capability.) Tap the Settings icon on the Home screen and then tap Video to configure your iPad for widescreen display on your TV.

Chatting with a View: FaceTime

The iPad also features front and back cameras and FaceTime, the app that enables you to video chat with other FaceTime users over a Wi-Fi or cellular link.

You need a Wi-Fi or a 3G/4G connection to use FaceTime — and the other person must have a Mac computer (running OS X Lion or later), an iPad 2 (or later), an iPod touch, or an iPhone 4/4S or 5 with FaceTime installed.

The first time you use FaceTime, you must enter your Apple ID and your e-mail address. The folks you chat with on the other end will use your e-mail address to call you via FaceTime.

After you sign in, follow these steps to make a call:

1. Tap a contact from the list.

FaceTime displays your Contacts list by default, but there are other methods of selecting someone to call. To display a list of recent calls, tap the Recent icon. You can also display a list of your favorite FaceTime callers by tapping the Favorites icon. To add someone as a favorite, tap the Add button (which carries a plus sign) at the top of the list.

2. When the call is accepted, you can see video from the caller's location.

Speak normally, and your caller should have no problem hearing you.

3. (Optional) During the call, switch between front and back cameras by tapping the Camera Switch icon.

You can use either camera with FaceTime — send video of yourself with the front camera, or share your surroundings while you talk using the back camera.

4. (Optional) To turn off audio from your side of the call, tap the Mute icon.

You can still hear audio from the caller's side of the conversation. Tap the Mute icon again to turn your microphone back on.

Press the Home button during a call, and you can run another app! You won't see the video, of course, but you can continue talking. When you're done with the other application, tap the green bar at the top of the window to return to FaceTime.

5. To hang up and end the call, tap the End icon.

If someone calls you with FaceTime, your iPad notifies you with a message. You can then choose to accept or dismiss the call.

Shooting Photos and Video

You can use the Camera app to take still photos and video using either of the cameras on the iPad. Tap the Camera icon, and you see a real-time display. To switch cameras between front and back, tap the Switch icon in the lower-right side of the screen. (Remember, you can also change the camera's orientation by simply rotating your iPad.) To switch between still photos and video, tap the Photo/Video icon in the lower-right corner of the screen.

As you probably already know, digital video takes up a lot of room on your iPad, so be selective when shooting video.

When you're ready to shoot, tap the Camera button at the center right side of the screen. You can also snap the photo (or start recording video) by pressing the Volume Up button on the side of your iPad. If you're shooting video, tap the Camera button again to stop recording (or press the Volume Up button again). To review your photos and video clips, tap the Review thumbnail at the bottom left of the screen. You can print and e-mail your handiwork, as well as use photos as wallpaper.

While reviewing your photos, tap the Slideshow button at the top of the screen for an instant professional-looking slideshow.

To add a little spice and special effects to your still photos, tap the Photo Booth icon on the Home screen. You can choose from eight different effects for your images. Again, you can switch between the front and back cameras. Tap the Camera button to shoot some out-of-this-world photos.

You can even shoot photos or video directly from your iPad's Lock screen! Drag the Camera icon upward to reveal the Camera app.

Beginning the iBook Story

To start reading electronic books on your iPad, you have to fetch the iBooks app in the App Store. (For more on the App Store, consult Chapter 6.)

As you might imagine, the app is free (like the Podcasts and iTunes U apps we mentioned earlier), and it comes with access to Apple's iBookstore, of which we have more to say later in this chapter. For now just know that it's an inviting place to browse and shop for books 24 hours a day. And, as a bonus for walking into this virtual bookstore, you'll receive a free electronic copy of *Winnie-the-Pooh.*

Your copy of A. A. Milne's classic and all the other books you purchase for your iPad library turn up on the handsome wooden bookshelf, shown in Figure 5-10. The following basics help you navigate the iBooks main screen:

- **Change the view:** If you'd prefer to view a list of your books rather than use this Bookshelf view, tap the List view button toward the upper-right corner of the screen (see Figure 5-10). In this view, you can sort the list by title, author, or category (as shown in Figure 5-11), or you can rearrange where books appear on the bookshelf.

- **Rearrange books on the bookshelf:** Tap Bookshelf from the List view and tap Edit (in the upper-right corner). Now press your finger against the icon to the right with the three horizontal lines of the book title you want to move. Drag the book up or down the list.

Open iBookstore

Tap cover to open a book

List view

Bookshelf view

Figure 5-10: You can read a book by its cover.

> ✏ **Remove a book from the bookshelf:** In the List view, tap Edit and then tap the circle to the left of the book title you want to remove. Then tap Delete. In the Bookshelf view, tap Edit and then tap the offending book cover to display the check mark. Then tap Delete.

Of course, here we are telling you how to get rid of a book before you've even had a chance to read it. How gauche. The next section helps you start reading.

Figure 5-11: Sort a list of your books by title, author, category, or bookshelf.

Reading a Book

You can start reading a book by tapping it on the bookshelf in your iPad library. The book leaps off the shelf and opens to either the beginning of the book or the place where you left off last time.

Even from the very title page, you can appreciate the color and beauty of Apple's app as well as the navigation tools, shown in Figure 5-12.

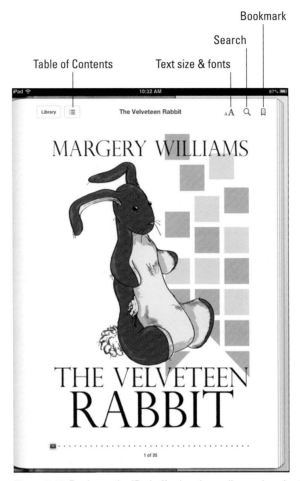

Figure 5-12: Books on the iPad offer handy reading and navigation tools.

While lounging around reading, and especially if you're lying down, we recommend that you use the screen rotation lock (described in Chapter 1) to stop the iPad from inadvertently rotating the display.

You ca.1 also take advantage of the iPad's VoiceOver feature to have the iPad read to you aloud. It may not be quite like having Mom or Dad read you to sleep, but it can be a potential godsend to those with impaired vision.

Turn pages

You've been turning pages in books your entire life, so you don't want this simple feat to become a complicated ordeal just because you're now reading electronically. It's not. You have no buttons to press.

Instead, to turn to the *next* page of a book, do any of the following:

- **Tap or flick your finger near the right margin of the page.**

- **Drag your finger near the margin,** and the page folds down as it turns, as if you were turning pages in a real book.

- **Drag down from the upper-right corner of the book,** and the page curls from that spot.

- **Drag up from the lower-right corner,** and it drags up from that spot.

- **Drag from the middle-right margin,** and the entire page curls.

To turn to the *previous* page in a book, tap, flick, or drag your finger in a similar fashion, except now do so closer to the left margin. You'll witness the same cool page-turning effects.

That's what happens, by default anyway. If you run the Settings app and tap iBooks under Apps on the left side of the screen, you have the option to go to the next page instead of the previous page when you tap near the left margin.

The iPad is smart, remembering where you left off. So if you close a book by tapping the Library button in the upper-left corner or by pressing the main Home button, you are automatically returned to this page when you reopen the book. It isn't necessary to bookmark the page (though you can, as we describe later in this chapter).

Jump to a specific page

When you're reading a book, you often want to go to a specific page. Here's how:

1. **Tap anywhere near the center of the page you're reading to summon page navigator controls (Figure 5-12), if they're not already visible.**

2. **Drag your finger along the slider at the bottom of the screen until the chapter and page number you want appear.**

3. **Release your finger and *voilà* — that's where you are in the book.**

Go to the table of contents

Books you read on your iPad have tables of contents, just like almost any other book. Here's how you use a table of contents on your iPad:

1. **With a book open on your iPad, tap the Table of Contents/Bookmark button near the top of the screen.**

   The Table of Contents screen shown in Figure 5-13 appears.

2. **Tap the chapter, title page, or another entry to jump to that page.**

   Alternatively, tap the Resume button that appears at the top left of the screen to return to the previous location in the book.

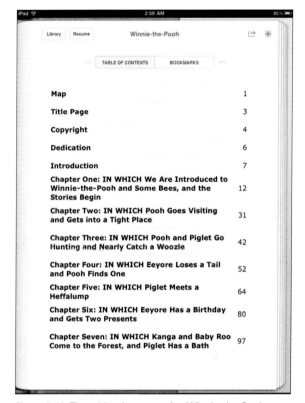

Figure 5-13: The table of contents for *Winnie-the-Pooh.*

Add bookmarks

On the iPad, moving to a particular location in an e-book is almost as simple as moving around a paper book. In some ways, e-books are simpler. For example, you don't need to bookmark where you left off in an e-book, because (as we explain in the earlier section "Turn pages") the iPad kindly returns you to the last page you were reading when you closed an e-book.

Still, occasionally, you want to bookmark a specific page so that you can easily find it again. To insert a bookmark on a page, display the navigation tools and tap the Ribbon icon at the top right. A fancy-looking red ribbon appears, indicating that you've bookmarked the page.

After you set a bookmark, here's what you can do with it:

✔ **To find the bookmark later,** tap the Table of Contents/ Bookmark button and then tap Bookmarks (if it's not already selected). Your bookmark is listed along with the chapter and page citations and the date you bookmarked the page. Tap to return to that page in the book.

✔ **To remove a bookmark,** tap the red bookmark ribbon on the page. Or from the bookmarks list, swipe your finger in either direction along a bookmark entry and tap the red Delete button that appears.

Change the type size and font

If you want to enlarge the typeface size (or make it smaller), here's how:

1. **Tap the Fonts button at the upper-right corner of the screen (refer to Figure 5-12).**

2. **Tap the uppercase *A*.**

   The text swells up right before your eyes so that you can pick a size you're comfortable with. To make it smaller, tap the lowercase *a* instead.

If you want to change the fonts, tap the Fonts button and then tap the font style you want to switch to. Your choices are Baskerville, Cochin, Georgia, Palatino, Times New Roman, and Verdana. We don't necessarily expect you to know what these look like just by the font names. Fortunately, you get to examine the change right before your eyes. The currently selected font style is indicated by a check mark.

Search inside and outside a book

If you want to find a passage in a book but just can't remember where it is, try searching for it. Here's how:

1. **Tap the magnifying glass Search icon to enter a search phrase on the virtual keyboard that slides up from the bottom.**

   All the occurrences in the book turn up in a window under the Search icon.

2. Tap one of the items to jump to that portion of the book.

You can also search Google or the Wikipedia online encyclo-
pedia using the buttons at the bottom of the search results.
If you do so, the iBooks app closes and the Safari browser
fires up Google or Wikipedia, with your search term already
entered.

If you search Google or Wikipedia in this fashion, you are for
the moment closing the iBooks application and opening Safari.
To return to the book you are reading, tap the iBooks icon
again to reopen the app, and you're brought back to the page
in the book where you left off.

Shopping for E-Books

The experience of browsing Apple's new iBookstore, although
certainly different from shopping at a brick-and-mortar store,
is equally pleasurable. Apple makes it a cinch to search for
books you want to read, and even lets you peruse a sample
prior to parting with your hard-earned dollars. To enter the
store, tap the Store button in the upper-left corner of your
virtual bookshelf or your library List view.

Many bestsellers cost $12.99, although some fetch $9.99 or
less. In fact, Apple even has a $9.99-or-less section, and free
selections are available.

Browsing the iBookstore

You have several ways to browse for books in the iBookstore.
The top half of the screen shows ever-changing ads for books
that fit a chosen category. But you can also browse the "New
In" row within the particular category you have in mind. To
show additional books in a row, flick the row to the left or
right. Tap See All for many more selections.

To choose another category of books, tap the Categories
button to summon the list. You have to scroll to see the
bottom of the list. Figure 5-14 illustrates a typical category list.

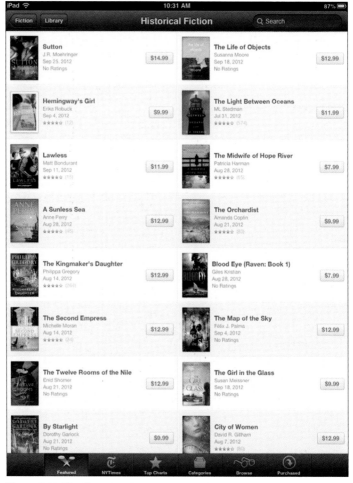

Figure 5-14: The Historical Fiction category list.

At the bottom of the screen, you also see the following icons:

✔ **Featured:** This is where we've been hanging out so far. Featured works are the books being promoted in the store. These may include popular titles from Oprah's Book Club or an author spotlight from the likes of *Twilight* writer Stephenie Meyer.

✔ **NYTimes:** Short for *The New York Times*, of course. These books make the newspaper's famous bestsellers lists, which are divided into the top fiction and nonfiction works. Again, you can scroll each row independently, or tap See All to view additional titles.

✏ **Top Charts:** Here Apple is showing you the most popular books in the iBookstore. You find a list for Top Paid Books and Top Free Books. Once more, you can see more than the top ten shown in each category by tapping Show More.

✏ **Browse:** Tap this icon to look through the store in a convenient list form (by authors or categories).

✏ **Purchased:** Tapping here shows you the books you've already bought. In this area, you can also check out your iTunes account information, tap a button that transports you to iTunes customer service, and redeem any iTunes gift cards or gift certificates. To re-download a book through iCloud, tap the iCloud icon next to the desired title. You can toggle between a display of all the books you've purchased and a display of only the books that haven't been downloaded on your iPad yet.

Searching the iBookstore

In the upper-right corner of the iBookstore is a search field, similar to the Search field you see in iTunes. Using the virtual keyboard, type in an author name or title to find the book you're looking for.

If you like freebies, search for the word *free* in the iBookstore. You'll find dozens of (mostly classic) books that cost nothing, and you won't even have to import them. See the section "Finding free books outside the iBookstore," later in this chapter for more places to find free books.

Deciding whether a book is worth it

To find out more about a book you come across in the iBookstore, you can check out the detail page and other readers' reviews or read a sample of the book. Follow these steps to navigate the detail page:

1. **In the iBookstore, tap the book's cover.**

   An information screen similar to the one shown for *Every Love Story Is a Ghost Story* in Figure 5-15 appears. You can see when the book was published, read a description, and more.

2. **Tap the Action icon (at the top-right corner of the screen) to share information on this book through Mail, Twitter, or Facebook.**

3. **Check out customer reviews and ratings. Tap Ratings and Reviews, then drag to scroll down the overlay and see all the reviews.**

   Throw in your own two cents if you've already read it by tapping Write a Review.

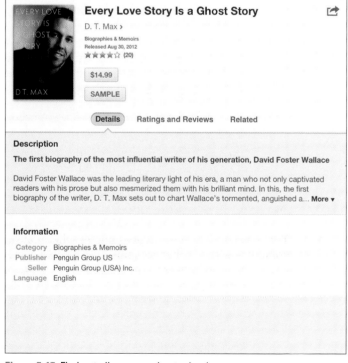

Figure 5-15: Find out all you can about a book.

Of course, the best thing you can do to determine whether a book is worth buying is to read a sample. Tap Sample, and the book cover almost immediately lands on your bookshelf. You can read it like any book, up until that juncture in the book where your free sample ends. Apple has placed a Buy button inside the pages of the book to make it easy to purchase it if you're hooked. The word *Sample* also appears on the cover, to remind you that this book isn't quite yours — yet.

Buying a book from the iBookstore

Assuming that the book exceeds your lofty standards and you are ready to purchase it, here's how to do so:

1. **Tap the price shown in the gray button on the book's information page.**

   The dollar amount disappears and the button becomes green and carries a Buy Book label. If you tap a free book instead, the button is labeled Get Book.

2. **Tap the Buy Book/Get Book button.**

3. **Enter your Apple ID password to proceed with the transaction.**

   The book appears on your bookshelf in an instant, ready for you to tap it and start reading.

Buying books beyond Apple

The business world is full of examples where one company competes with another on some level only to work with it as a partner on another. When the iPad first burst onto the scene in early April 2010, pundits immediately compared it to Amazon's Kindle, the market-leading electronic reader. Sure, the iPad had the larger screen and color, but Kindle had a few bragging points, too, including longer battery life (up to about two weeks versus about ten hours for the iPad), a lighter weight, and a larger selection of books in its online bookstore.

But Amazon has long said it wants Kindle books to be available for all sorts of electronic platforms, and the iPad, like the iPhone and iPod touch before it, is no exception. So we recommend taking a look at the free Kindle app for the iPad, especially if you've already purchased a number of books in Amazon's Kindle Store and want access to that wider selection of titles.

Meanwhile, we haven't tried them all, and we know it's hard enough competing against Apple (or Amazon). But we'd be selling our readers short if we didn't at least mention that you can find several other e-book-type apps for the iPad in the App Store. As this book goes to press, you can have a look at the following apps, just to name a few:

✔ CloudReaders from Satoshi Nakajima (free)

✔ Kobo from Kobo Inc. (free)

✔ Stanza from Lexcycle (free)

Finding free books outside the iBookstore

Apple supports a technical standard called *ePub,* the underlying technology behind thousands of free public-domain books. You can import these to the iPad without shopping in the iBookstore. Such titles must be *DRM*-free, which means they are free of digital rights restrictions.

To import ePub titles, you have to download them to your PC or Mac (assuming that they're not already there) and then sync them to the iPad through iTunes.

You can find ePub titles at numerous cyberspace destinations, among them

✔ Feedbooks (www.feedbooks.com)

✔ Google Books (http://books.google.com) (Google has a downloadable app)

✔ Project Gutenberg (www.gutenberg.us)

✔ Smashwords (www.smashwords.com)

Perusing with Newsstand

With the success of iBooks, Apple decided to add a similar app to the iPad for reading magazine and newspaper subscriptions — and *Newsstand* was born. You'll notice the similarities immediately because Newsstand uses the same "virtual shelf" navigation system as iBooks. However, you don't use iBookstore to purchase your periodicals; instead, a separate section of the App Store has been added just for this purpose.

To shop for a subscription, tap the Newsstand icon and then tap the Store button. The App Store appears, already set to display periodical subscriptions. Like any other type of iPad app, you can search or browse the titles, or tap a subscription thumbnail to see additional information. When you've decided on a subscription, tap the price/Free button. After the periodical is downloaded into Newsstand, simply tap the cover to begin reading.

Ah, but by definition, a periodical needs periodic updating! That's where the fun begins within Newsstand: The app automatically downloads the new issues of your subscriptions and indicates that new content has arrived by displaying an alert! (Look for the red circle that highlights how many new issues you have to read.)

Chapter 6
Gotta Love Those Apps!

* *

In This Chapter

▶ Browsing for cool apps

▶ Searching for specific apps

▶ Getting apps onto your iPad

▶ Managing iPad apps

▶ Socializing with Facebook, Twitter, and other social media apps

* *

*O*ne of the best things about the iPad is that you can download and install apps created by third parties, which is to say apps not created by Apple (the first party) or you (the second party). At the time of this writing, more than 300,000 apps are available in the iTunes App Store. Many apps are free, but others cost money. Some apps are useful, but others are lame. Some apps are perfectly well behaved, but others quit unexpectedly (or worse). The point is simply that some apps are better than others.

In this chapter, we take a broad look at apps you can use with your iPad. You discover how to find apps on your computer or your iPad, and you find some basics for managing your apps.

Tapping the Magic of Apps

Apps enable you to use your iPad as a game console, a streaming Netflix player, a recipe finder, a sketchbook, and much, much more. You can run three different categories of apps on your iPad:

  ✔ **Apps made exclusively for the iPad:** This is the newest kind, so you find fewer of these than the other two types.

These apps won't run on an iPhone or iPod touch, so don't bother to try them on either device. Depending on how recently the app was written, it may also support the high-resolution screen on the latest iPad.

✓ **Apps made to work properly on an iPad, an iPhone, or an iPod touch:** This type of app can run on any of the three devices at full resolution.

✓ **Apps made for the iPhone and iPod touch:** These apps run on your iPad, but only at the smaller iPhone/iPod touch resolution rather than the larger resolution of your iPad.

You can double the size of an iPhone/iPod touch app by tapping the little 2x button in the lower-right corner of the screen; to return it to its native size, tap the 1x button.

Frankly, most iPhone/iPod apps look pretty good at 2x size, but we've seen a few that have jagged graphics and don't look as nice. Still, with 300,000 or more to choose from, we're sure that you can find a few that make you happy.

Figure 6-1 shows you what this looks like.

Figure 6-1: iPhone or iPod touch apps run at a smaller size (left) but can be "blown up" to double size (right).

You can obtain and install apps for your iPad in two ways:

✔ On your computer

✔ On your iPad

In the days before iCloud, if you downloaded an app on your computer, it wasn't available on your iPad until you synced the iPad with your computer. In iOS 5 (and later), however, apps that you download on your iPad or computer are automatically pushed to your other iOS devices via iCloud.

To use the App Store on your iPad (or to transfer data wirelessly using iCloud), it must be connected to the Internet.

But before you can use the App Store on your iPad or your computer, you first need an Apple ID. If you don't already have one, we suggest that you launch iTunes on your computer, click Sign In near the upper-right corner of the iTunes window, and then click Create Apple ID and follow the onscreen instructions.

Let's put it this way: If you don't have an Apple ID, you can't download a single cool app or iBook for your iPad (not to mention movies, music, and the other goodies). Even the free ones are off-limits!

Using Your Computer to Find Apps

Okay, start by finding cool iPad apps using iTunes on your computer. Follow these steps:

1. **Launch iTunes.**

2. **Click the iTunes Store link in the sidebar on the left.**

3. **Click the Apps link at the top of the window.**

   The iTunes App Store appears, as shown in Figure 6-2.

4. **(Optional) If you want to look only for apps designed to run at the full resolution of your iPad, click the iPad button at the top of the window.**

iTunes Store (in sidebar)   iPad tab   Search

See All links   Apps Store

Figure 6-2: The iTunes App Store, in all its glory.

Browsing the App Store from your computer

After you have the iTunes App Store on your screen, you have a couple of options for exploring its virtual aisles. This section introduces the various "departments" available from the main screen.

The main departments are featured in the middle of the screen, and ancillary departments appear on either side of them. We start with the ones in the middle (although not all are visible in Figure 6-2, and some are added during product launches, like the iPhone 5):

✔ **New and Noteworthy:** This department includes apps that are — what else? — new and noteworthy.

Look to the right of the words *New and Noteworthy.* See the words *See All?* That's a link; if you click it, you see *all* apps in this department on a single screen. Or, you can click and drag the scrollbar to the right to see more icons.

- ✓ **What's Hot:** This department appears below New and Noteworthy and includes apps popular with other iPad users.

- ✓ **Staff Favorites:** This department appears below What's Hot.

Apple has a habit of redecorating the iTunes Stores every so often, so allow us to apologize in advance if things aren't exactly as described here when you visit.

You also see display ads for featured apps between each department.

Three other departments appear to the right, under the Top Charts heading: Top Paid Apps, one of our favorite departments; Top Free Apps; and Top Grossing Apps. The number one app in each department displays both its icon and its name; the next nine apps show text links only.

Finally, the Apps link near the top of the screen is also a drop-down menu (as are most of the other department links to its left and right). If you click and hold on most of these department links, a menu with a list of the department's categories appears. For example, if you click and hold on the App Store link, you can choose specific categories such as Books, Entertainment, and others from the drop-down menu, enabling you to bypass the App Store home page and go directly to that category.

Using the Search field

Browsing the screen is helpful, but if you know exactly what you're looking for, we have good news: There's a faster way! Just type a word or phrase into the Search field in the upper-right corner of the main iTunes window, as shown in Figure 6-3, and then press Enter or Return to initiate the search.

Your search results are segregated into categories — one of which is iPad Apps. And, here's even more good news: If you click the See All link to the right of the words *iPad Apps*, all the iPad apps that match your search word or phrase appear on a single screen.

See All link   Search

Figure 6-3: I want to use my iPad as a flashlight, so I searched for the word *flashlight*.

The little triangle to the right of each item's price is another drop-down menu. This one lets you give this app to someone as a gift, add it to your wish list, send an e-mail to a friend with a link to it, copy the link to this product to the Clipboard so that you can paste it elsewhere, or share this item on Facebook or Twitter.

Getting more information about an app

Now that you know how to find apps in the App Store, this section delves a little deeper and shows you how to find out more about an application that interests you.

To find out more about an application icon, a featured app, or a text link on any of the iTunes App Store screens, just click it. A detail screen like the one shown in Figure 6-4 appears.

This screen should tell you most of what you need to know about the application, such as basic product information and a narrative description, what's new in this version, the language it's presented in, and the system requirements to run the app. In the following sections, you take a closer look at the various areas on the screen.

Requirements Rating

Click More
to see full description

Figure 6-4: The detail screen for SketchBook Pro, a nifty drawing and painting app for your iPad.

Finding the full app description

Notice the blue More link in the lower-right corner of the Description section? Click it to see a much longer description of the app.

Bear in mind that the application description on this screen was written by the application's developer and may be somewhat biased.

Understanding the app rating

Notice that this application is rated 4+, as you can see below the Buy App button, near the top of the screen shown in Figure 6-4. The rating means that this app contains no objectionable material. Here are the other possible ratings:

✔ **9+:** May contain mild or infrequent occurrences of cartoon, fantasy, or realistic violence; or infrequent or mild mature, suggestive, or horror-themed content that may not be suitable for children under the age of 9.

✔ **12+:** May contain infrequent mild language; frequent or intense cartoon, fantasy, or realistic violence; mild or infrequent mature or suggestive themes; or simulated gambling that may not be suitable for children under the age of 12.

✔ **17+:** May contain frequent and intense offensive language; frequent and intense cartoon, fantasy, or realistic violence; mature, frequent, and intense mature, suggestive, or horror-themed content; sexual content; nudity; or depictions of alcohol, tobacco, or drugs that may not be suitable for children under the age of 17. You must be at least 17 years old to purchase games with this rating.

Following related links

Just below the application description, notice the collection of useful links (typically including the developer's website and online support). We urge you to explore these links at your leisure.

Checking requirements and device support for the app

Last but not least, remember the three different categories of apps we mentioned earlier in the chapter, in the section "Tapping the Magic of Apps"? If you look under the rating (Rated 4+), you can see the requirements for this particular app. Because it reads "Compatible with iPad. Requires iPhone OS 5.0 or later" and doesn't mention the iPhone or iPod touch, this app falls into the first category — apps made exclusively for the iPad. (The listing should also identify whether the app supports the Retina display if you have one.) Another clue that it falls into the first category is that it says "iPad Screenshots" above the three pictures shown in Figure 6-4.

If it belonged to the second or third categories — apps made to work properly on an iPad, iPhone, or iPod touch, or apps made for the iPhone or iPod touch — it would say "Compatible with iPhone, iPod touch, and iPad" rather than "Compatible with iPad."

Now you're probably wondering how you can tell whether an app falls into the second or third category. One clue is to look at the screen shots. If you see two tabs — iPhone and iPad — after the word *Screenshots,* the app is the second type and will work at the full resolution of an iPad, iPhone, or iPod touch. If you don't see the two tabs and it reads "iPhone Screenshots," the app is the third type and will only run at iPhone or iPod touch resolution on your iPad.

One way to ensure that you are looking only for apps that take advantage of your iPad's big screen is to click the iPad button at the top of the front page of the App Store (shown in Figure 6-2). All the apps displayed under the iPad tab are of the first or second type and can run at the full resolution of your iPad.

Downloading an app

This part is simple. When you find an application you want to try, click its Free App or Buy App button. When you do so, you'll have to log on to your iTunes Store account, even if the app is free.

After you log on, the app begins downloading. When it's finished, it appears in the Apps section of your iTunes library, as shown in Figure 6-5.

With iCloud, downloading an app to your iTunes library on your computer will automatically push it to your iPad. However, if your hardware doesn't support iCloud, you have to sync your iPad before the application will be available on it.

By the way, if your iTunes App library doesn't look like ours (with big icons in a grid pattern), try clicking the third icon in the group of four icons to the right of the Search field near the top of the iTunes window.

Figure 6-5: Apps that you download appear in the Apps section of your iTunes library.

Using Your iPad to Find Apps

Finding apps with your iPad is almost as easy as finding them by using iTunes. The only requirement is that you have an Internet connection of some sort — Wi-Fi or wireless data network — so that you can access the iTunes App Store and browse, search, download, and install apps.

Browsing the App Store on your iPad

To get started, tap the App Store icon on your iPad's Home screen. After you launch the App Store, you see five icons at the bottom of the screen, representing five ways to interact with the store, as shown in Figure 6-6. The first three icons at the bottom of the screen — Featured, Charts, and Genius — offer three ways to browse the virtual shelves of the App Store. (The fourth and fifth icons we cover a little later, in the section "Updating and re-downloading an app.")

Here are descriptions of the three icons you use for browsing the App Store:

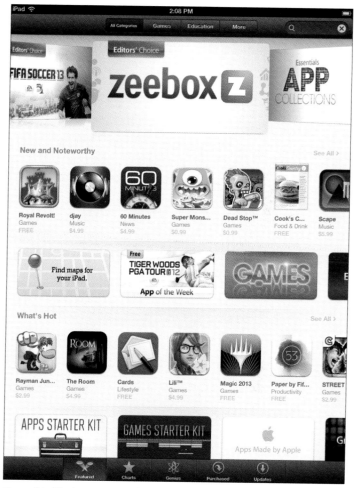

Figure 6-6: The icons across the bottom represent the five sections of the App Store.

✔ **Featured:** Displays a number of scrolling rows, each with similar apps: New and Noteworthy and What's Hot, for example (see Figure 6-6). Note that these featured rows may change from time to time.

✔ **Genius:** Displays apps that you may like based on the apps that you've already installed.

 ✒ **Charts:** Offers lists of the Top Paid iPad Apps and the Top Free iPad Apps. These are, of course, the most popular apps that either cost money or don't.

At the top of the App Store screen are a series of Category buttons. Tap one to see a list of apps in that category, or tap More to see the full category list.

Most rows in the App Store display more apps than can fit on the screen at once. Tap the **See All** link at the top of most rows to (what else?) see all the apps in that row on the same screen.

Using the Search field

If you know exactly what you're looking for, rather than simply browsing, you can tap the Search field in the upper-right corner of the screen and type a word or phrase; then tap the Search key on the keyboard to initiate the search.

Finding details about an app

Now that you know how to find apps in the App Store, this section shows you how to find out more about a particular application. After tapping an app icon as you browse the store or in a search result, you see a detail screen like the one shown in Figure 6-7.

The application description on this screen was written by the developer and may be somewhat biased.

The information you find on the detail screen on your iPad is similar to that in the iTunes screen you see on your computer. The links, rating, and requirements simply appear in slightly different places on your iPad screen. (See the section "Getting more information about an app," earlier in this chapter, for explanations of the main onscreen items.)

The reviews section differs most from the computer version. You'll see the star rating toward the top of the detail screen. Tap Ratings and Reviews to access the reviews for the app.

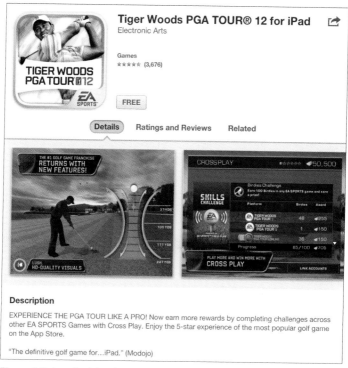

Figure 6-7: A typical detail screen for an iPad app.

Downloading an app

To download an application to your iPad, follow these steps:

1. **Tap the price button near the top of its detail screen.**

   The gray price button is then replaced by a green rectangle that says Install App.

2. **Tap the Install App button.**

3. **When prompted, type your Apple ID password.**

   After you do, the App Store closes and you see the Home screen where the new application's icon will reside. The new app's icon is slightly dimmed and has the word *Loading* beneath it, with a blue progress bar near its bottom to indicate how much of the app remains to be downloaded, as shown in Figure 6-8.

4. **(Optional) If the app is rated 17+, click OK in the warning screen that appears after you type your password to confirm that you're over 17 before the app downloads.**

Progress bar

Figure 6-8: The app above the Photos icon is downloading; the blue progress bar indicates that it's a quarter done.

iCloud comes to the rescue again! The application will automatically appear in your iTunes library on your Mac or PC — no old-fashioned syncing with a USB cable necessary!

Updating and re-downloading an app

As mentioned earlier in this chapter, every so often the developer of an iPad application releases an update. If an update awaits you, a little number in a circle appears on the Updates icon at the bottom of the screen. Follow these steps to update your apps:

1. **Tap the Updates icon if any of your apps need updating.**

   If you tap the Updates icon and see (in the middle of the screen) a message that says All Apps are Up-to-Date, none of the apps on your iPad require an update at this time. If apps need updating, they appear with Update buttons next to them.

2. **Tap the Update button that appears next to any app to update it.**

   If more than one application needs updating, you can update them all at once by tapping the Update All button in the upper-right corner of the screen.

Updating an application does not require you to enter your Apple ID password.

After you've paid for an app, you can download it again if you need to, and you don't have to pay for it again. To re-download an app, open the App Store on your iPad and tap the Purchased icon at the bottom of the screen. The App Store displays all the apps you've downloaded in the past. To fine a specific app, use the Search box in the upper-right corner of the screen, or tap the Sort By field to display apps sorted by Most Recent or App Name.

If an app is currently installed, it bears the Installed label. You can re-download an app that you deleted by tapping the iCloud icon next to the app name — the App Store prompts you for your Apple ID.

Working with Apps

Most of what you need to know about apps involves simply installing third-party apps on your iPad. However, you might find it helpful to know how to delete an app or rearrange your apps.

Deleting an app

You can delete an app in two ways: in iTunes on your computer or directly from your iPad.

To delete an app in iTunes, click Apps in the sidebar and then do one of the following:

- Click the app to select it and press the Backspace or Delete key on the keyboard.
- Click the app to select it and then choose Edit↔Delete.
- Right-click the app and choose Delete.

After taking any of the actions in this list, you see a confirmation dialog box that asks whether you're sure that you want to remove the selected application. Click the Move to Trash button to remove the app from your iTunes library, as well as from any iPad that syncs with your iTunes library. (This is the best option because iTunes reclaims the space that the app was taking on your computer's hard drive.) Click Cancel to keep the app.

Here's how to delete an application on your iPad:

1. **Press and hold any icon until all the icons begin to "wiggle."**

2. **Tap the little *x* in the upper-left corner of the application that you want to delete.**

   A dialog box appears, as shown in Figure 6-9, informing you that deleting this application also deletes all its data.

3. **Tap the Delete button.**

Figure 6-9: Tap an app's little *x*, and then tap Delete to remove the app from your iPad.

To stop the icons from wiggling, just press the Home or Sleep/ Wake button.

Deleting an app from your iPad this way doesn't get rid of it permanently. It remains in your iTunes library (and takes up space on your computer's hard drive) until you delete it from iTunes, as described earlier in this chapter. Put another way: Even though you deleted the app from your iPad, it's still in your iTunes library. If you want to get rid of an app for good after you delete it on your iPad, you must also delete it from your iTunes library.

Arranging app icons

You also make icons wiggle to move them around on the screen or move them from page to page. To rearrange wiggling icons, press and drag them one at a time. If you drag an icon to the left or right edge of the screen, it moves to the next or previous Home screen. You can also drag two additional icons to the dock (where Safari, Mail, Photos, and Music live) and have six apps available from every Home screen.

Socializing with Social Media Apps

Your iPad doesn't include any specific social media apps right out of the box, but you can add free client apps for the major social media networks including Facebook, Myspace, Twitter, and Apple's Game Center.

iOS 6 also has support for both Twitter and Facebook built into many of the Apple iPad apps — you can tweet or post directly from Safari, Photos, Camera, and Maps. Things get even better: You only need to enter your Twitter and Facebook username and password once within Settings, and your iPad signs you in automatically ever after! You can choose to add your location to your tweets and posts, too.

As of this writing, only Game Center, Facebook, and Twitter offer client apps that run natively on the iPad. Although we are certain Myspace will get around to releasing a bigger, better, iPad-friendly app soon, for now all we can show you is the iPhone version of the apps running at iPhone resolution.

Note that you don't necessarily need an app to participate in social networking. Three of the four networks we mentioned can be fully utilized using Safari on your iPad. And frankly, unlike the iPhone, where the Safari experience was hampered by the tiny screen and keyboard, all three websites are eminently usable on your iPad. So, if you want to check them out and don't feel like downloading their apps, here are their URLs:

- **Facebook:** www.facebook.com
- **Myspace:** www.myspace.com
- **Twitter:** http://twitter.com

Game Center

Game Center is the odd duck of the bunch. As we mentioned, unlike the others, there is no Game Center website; you have to use the Game Center app that came with your iPad. And unlike the others, which are broad-based and aimed at anyone and everyone, Game Center is designed for a specific segment of the iPad (and Mac, and iPhone, and iPad touch) universe: namely users who have one or more games that support Game Center.

Game Center acts as a match-up service, letting you challenge your friends or use Auto-Match to challenge a stranger who also happens to be looking for someone to play against. Figure 6-10 shows Bob about to initiate a two-player game of Flight Control HD.

Of course, to make a social network like Game Center a success, there needs to be lots of games that support Game Center. And therein lies the rub. Because Game Center is relatively new (born in late 2010), many older games don't include Game Center support.

On the positive side, the ones that do support Game Center include such top sellers as Angry Birds, Real Racing HD, Pinball HD, and the World Series of Poker.

Figure 6-10: Invite a stranger to play (Auto-Match) or click the Invite Friend button to challenge a friend.

Facebook

The Facebook iPad app, shown in Figure 6-11, makes it easy to access the most popular Facebook features with a single finger tap — which ties in well with the Facebook sharing options that Apple has integrated into iOS 6.

If you're used to Facebook within your browser window, why switch? As we mentioned before, you may prefer to view your

Facebook Live Feed in Safari rather than in the Facebook iPad app. On the other hand, Safari can't provide push notifications for Facebook events such as messages, wall posts, friend requests and confirmations, photo tags, events, and comments. The iPad app, however, does all that and more.

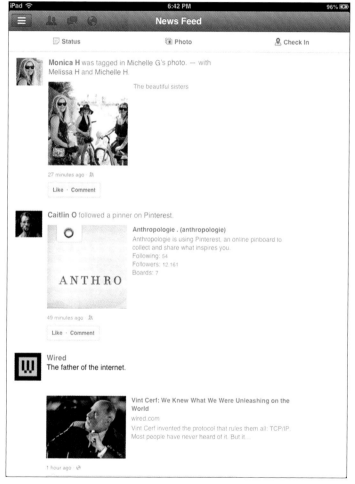

Figure 6-11: A Facebook News Feed as seen in the Facebook iPad app.

The bottom line is that there's nothing to prevent having the best of both worlds. So if you're a heavy Facebook user, consider using the Facebook iPad app for some things (such as push notifications and status updates) and Safari for others (such as reading your Wall or Live Feeds).

Myspace

As of this moment, an iPad version isn't available. And as far as we can see, you don't have any reason to use the iPhone app 'cause it doesn't even offer push notifications (as the Facebook iPad app does).

Take a look at the Myspace app in Figure 6-12 and then decide.

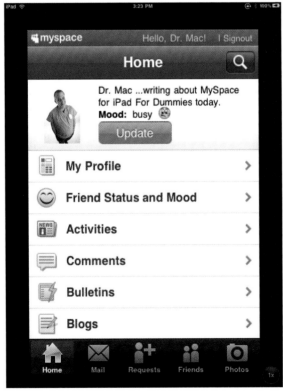

Figure 6-12: A Myspace home page as seen in the Myspace iPhone app.

We reserve the right to say something nice about the Myspace iPad app if they introduce one. But for now we think you'll enjoy interacting with Myspace more if you use Safari.

Twitter

Twitter puts a slightly different spin on social networking. Unlike Facebook or Myspace, it doesn't try to be encompassing or offer dozens of features, hoping that some of them will appeal to you. Instead, Twitter does one thing and does it well. That thing is letting its users post short messages called *tweets* quickly and easily from a variety of platforms including web browsers, mobile phones, smartphones, and other devices.

Twitter users then have the option of "following" any other Twitter user's tweets. The result is a stream of short messages like the ones seen in Figure 6-13. Apple has recognized Twitter's success by integrating support for tweeting in a number of iPad apps (the most obvious being Safari, Photos, and Maps).

Just how short are tweets? Glad you asked. You're limited to a mere 140 characters. That's barely longer than this Tip. So be as concise as possible.

Figure 6-13: The official Twitter iPad app as seen through the eyes of Bob (@LeVitus).

Chapter 7

Setting You Straight on Settings

Settings is kind of the makeover factory for the iPad. You open Settings by tapping its Home screen icon, and from there, you can do things such as change the tablet's background or wallpaper and specify Google, Bing, or Yahoo! as the search engine of choice. You can also alter security settings in Safari, tailor e-mail to your liking (among other modifications), and get a handle on how to fetch or push new data.

The Settings area on the iPad is roughly analogous to the Control Panel in Windows and System Preferences on a Mac.

Viewing the Settings Screen

When you first open Settings, you'll see a display that looks something like Figure 7-1, with a scrollable list on the left side of the screen and a panel on the right that corresponds to whichever setting is highlighted in blue. We say "something like this" because the Settings on your iPad may differ slightly from those of your neighbor's.

One other general thought to keep in mind: If a greater-than symbol (>) appears to the right of a listing, it is telling you that the listing has a bunch of options. Throughout this chapter, you tap the > symbol to check out those options.

Figure 7-1: Presenting your list of settings.

As you scroll to the bottom of the list on the left, you come to all the settings that pertain to some of the specific third-party apps you've added to the iPad (see Chapter 7). Everybody has a different collection of apps on his or her iPad, so any settings related to those programs will also obviously be different.

Flying with Sky-High Settings

Your iPad offers settings to keep you on the good side of air-traffic communications systems. Using a cellular radio or Wi-Fi networking on most airplanes is a no-no. But there's nothing verboten about using an iPad on a plane to listen to music, watch videos, and peek at pictures — at least, after the craft has reached cruising altitude.

So how do you take advantage of the iPad's built-in iPod (among other capabilities) at 30,000 feet while temporarily turning off your wireless gateway to e-mail and Internet functions? The answer is, by turning on Airplane mode.

To do so, merely tap Airplane mode on the Settings screen to display On (rather than Off).

That act disables each of the iPad's wireless radios: Wi-Fi, EDGE, 3G/4G, and Bluetooth, as well as the location hardware used by Maps and other apps. While your iPad is in Airplane mode, you can't surf the web, get a map location, send or receive e-mails, stream video, sync contacts, use iTunes or the App Store, connect with iCloud, or do anything else that requires an Internet connection. If there's a silver lining here, it's that the iPad's long-lasting battery ought to last even longer — good news if the flight you're on is taking you half-way around the planet.

 The appearance of a tiny Airplane icon on the status bar at the top of the screen reminds you that Airplane mode is turned on. Just remember to turn it off when you're back on the ground.

If you plug the iPad into an iPod accessory that isn't neces-sarily compatible because of possible interference from the iPad's wireless radios, it offers to turn on Airplane mode for you.

Controlling Wi-Fi Connections

As you may already know, Wi-Fi is typically the fastest wire-less network you can use to surf the web, send e-mail, and perform other Internet tricks on the iPad. You use the Wi-Fi setting to determine which Wi-Fi networks are available to you and which one to exploit based on its signal.

Tap Wi-Fi so that the setting is on and all Wi-Fi networks in range are displayed, as shown in Figure 7-2.

Tap the Wi-Fi switch to off when you don't have access to a network and don't want to drain the battery.

A signal-strength indicator can help you choose the network to connect to if more than one is listed; tap the appropriate Wi-Fi network when you reach a decision. If a network is password-protected, you see a Lock icon.

You can also turn the Ask to Join Networks setting on or off. Networks that the iPad are already familiar with are joined automatically, regardless of which one you choose. If the Ask feature is off and no known networks are available, you have to manually select a new network. If the Ask feature is on, you're asked before joining a new network. Either way, you see a list with the same Wi-Fi networks in range.

If you used a particular network automatically in the past but you no longer want your iPad to join it, tap the > symbol next to the network in question (within Wi-Fi settings) and then tap Forget This Network. The iPad develops a quick case of selec-tive amnesia.

Figure 7-2: Checking out your Wi-Fi options.

In some instances, you have to supply other technical information about a network you hope to glom on to. You encounter a bunch of nasty-sounding terms: DHCP, BootP, Static, IP Address, Subnet Mask, Router, DNS, Search Domains, client ID, HTTP Proxy, and Renew Lease. (At least this last one has nothing to do with renting an apartment or the vehicle you're driving.) Chances are that none of this info is on the tip of your tongue — but that's okay. For one thing, it's a good bet that you'll never need to know this stuff. What's more, even if you *do* have to fill in or adjust these settings, a network administrator or techie friend can probably help you out.

Sometimes, you may want to connect to a network that's closed and not shown on the Wi-Fi list. If that's the case, tap Other and use the keyboard to enter the network name. Then tap to choose the type of security setting the network is using (if any). Your choices are WEP, WPA, WPA2, WPA Enterprise, and WPA2 Enterprise. Again, it's not exactly the friendliest terminology in the world, but we figure that someone nearby can lend a hand.

If no Wi-Fi network is available, you have to rely on 3G, 4G/LTE, or EDGE if you have the Wi-Fi + 3G/4G model. If you don't or you're out of reach of a cellular network, you can't rocket into cyberspace until you regain access to a network.

Settings for Your Senses

The next bunch of settings control what the iPad looks and sounds like.

Brightening your day

Who doesn't want a bright, vibrant screen? Alas, the brightest screens exact a trade-off: Before you drag the brightness slider shown in Figure 7-3 to the max, remember that brighter screens sap the life from your battery more quickly. The control appears when Brightness & Wallpaper is highlighted.

We recommend tapping the Auto-Brightness control so that it's on. The control automatically adjusts the screen according to the lighting environment in which you're using the iPad while at the same time being considerate of your battery.

Figure 7-3: Sliding this control adjusts screen brightness.

Wallpaper

Choosing wallpaper is a neat way to dress up the iPad according to your aesthetic preferences. You can sample the pretty patterns and designs that the iPad has already chosen for you as follows:

1. **Tap the thumbnails shown when you highlight the Brightness & Wallpaper setting. (Refer to Figure 7-3.)**

2. **Choose an image.**

   You can choose a favorite picture from your photo albums or select one of the gorgeous images that Apple has supplied, as shown in Figure 7-4.

Figure 7-4: Choosing a masterpiece background.

3. **Tap one of the following options to set where your wallpaper appears:**

- Set Lock Screen makes your selected image the wallpaper of choice when the iPad is locked.

- Set Home Screen makes the wallpaper decorate only your Home screen.

- Set Both makes your image the wallpaper for locked and Home screens.

From Settings, you can also turn your iPad into an animated picture frame while it's locked. Tap the Picture Frame setting on the left to see the options. Choose which transition you prefer (a slow dissolve between photos or a nifty animated folding origami effect). You can set a delay between photos and optionally "zoom in" on faces in the photos that your iPad can detect. Your iPad can optionally shuffle photos that it displays. Finally, choose whether your iPad should display all photos or a specific album.

When your iPad is locked, tap the picture frame icon (which looks like a flower in a frame) to start or stop Picture Frame mode.

Sounds

Consider the Sounds settings, found in the Settings list to the left, the iPad's soundstage. You can turn audio alerts on or off for a variety of functions: new e-mail, sent mail, texts, tweets, reminder alerts, and calendar alerts. You can also decide whether you want to hear lock sounds and keyboard clicks.

To raise the decibel level of alerts, drag the volume slider to the right. Drag in the opposite direction to bring down the noise.

An alternative way to adjust sounds (as the iPad so often offers alternatives): You can use the physical Volume buttons on the side of the iPad for this purpose, as long as you're not already using the iPad's iPod to listen to music or watch video.

Side Switch

Tap the General settings item to display the Use Side Switch To setting. The default mode, Mute, silences system sounds. However, tap Lock Rotation, and your side switch can now prevent your iPad from changing orientations (no matter how you hold it).

Chapter 8

Accessorizing Your iPad

In This Chapter

▶ Covering your iPad

▶ Finding an alternative keyboard

▶ Exploring your connection options (camera, TV, and projector)

▶ Adding a spare charger

▶ Seeking out the best headphones and speakers

▶ Protecting your iPad screen

▶ Giving your iPad a leg to stand on

*A*pple and several other companies are all too happy to outfit your iPad with extra doodads, from wireless keyboards and stands to battery chargers and carrying cases.

A bevy of accessories fit perfectly into the iPad's not-so-old 30-pin dock connector. And each week, new accessories compatible with the new Lightning connector become available, from both Apple and third-party vendors. Whichever connector your iPad has, as long as you have the right cable or adapter, you might even try to plug the battery chargers or other iPod or iPhone accessories you have laying around into the iPad. No guarantee that these will work, but they probably will. And you have nothing to lose by trying.

One thing is certain: If you see a "Made for iPad" label on the package, the developer is certifying that an electronic accessory has been designed to connect specifically to the iPad and meets performance standards established by Apple.

Having a dock connector on-board means, of course, that you can count on seeing the continuing arrival of myriad accessories for the iPad, beyond those we mention in this chapter. So keep on the lookout: It's a fair bet you'll find some neat stuff from such usual suspects as Belkin and Griffin, as well as from startups whose names aren't familiar.

We start this accessories chapter with the options that carry Apple's own logo and conclude with worthwhile extras from other companies.

Adding a Case

The thing about accessories is that half the time you wish they weren't accessories at all. You wish they came in the box. Among the things we would have liked to have seen included with the iPad was a protective case.

Alas, it wasn't to be, but you can find cases aplenty just the same, and you can read about Apple's here, and other cases later in this chapter.

Apple's basic entry in this category, the Smart Cover, isn't technically a full case — it only covers the front of your iPad (second-generation or later). However, the lightweight $39 Smart Cover has specially designed magnets that align and hold it to the front of your iPad. When you remove the Smart Cover, your iPad wakes up automatically, and it goes to sleep automatically when you replace the Smart Cover. Finally, the versatile Smart Cover folds into two stands: one that makes typing on the virtual keyboard much easier, and one that acts as an easel for watching movies or displaying photos. At $39 for the polyurethane model and $69 for the leather model, the Smart Cover is superbly designed minimalism.

Apple also offers a Smart Case that protects both the front and the back of the device, with the same folding stands and sleep control. The Smart Case is $49 in polyurethane.

Wrapping Your iPad in Third-Party Cases

Much as we like the Apple Smart Cover and Smart Case, here are some other vendors of iPad cases:

↙ **Abas** (www.abas.net)

↙ **Targus** (www.targus.com)

↙ **Griffin Technology** (www.griffintechnology.com)

↙ **iLuv** (www.i-luv.com)

↙ **Hard Candy Cases** (www.hardcandycases.com)

If you decide on a third-party case, verify first that you can use Apple cables and devices without having to remove the iPad from the case. Let's face it: slipping your iPad out of a case over and over is the definition of *hassle*. Also, it's important to note that a case made for one iPad model will probably not be an exact fit for a different iPad model, so make certain you're buying the right case first.

Exploring Keyboard Alternatives

We think the various virtual keyboards that pop up just as you need them on the iPad are perfectly fine for shorter typing tasks, whether it's composing e-mails or tapping out a few notes. For most longer assignments, however, we writers are more comfortable pounding away on a real-deal physical keyboard, and we suspect you feel the same way.

Fortunately, a physical keyboard for the iPad is an easy addition. Apple sells a wireless keyboard for a mere $69.

The Apple Wireless Keyboard is a way to use a top-notch aluminum physical keyboard without having to tether it to the iPad. It operates from up to 30 feet away from the iPad via Bluetooth. Which begs us to ask, can you see the iPad screen from 30 feet away?

As with any Bluetooth device that the iPad makes nice with, you have to pair your wireless keyboard to your iPad.

The Bluetooth keyboard takes two AA batteries. It's smart about power management, too; it powers itself down when you stop using it to avoid draining those batteries. It wakes up when you start typing.

If you use a backpack, briefcase, messenger bag, or even a large purse, there's almost certainly room for the Apple Wireless Keyboard.

Though we haven't tested any models, the latest iPad ought to work fine with a non–Apple Bluetooth keyboard, as long as the keyboard supports Bluetooth 2.1 + EDR technology.

Connecting a Camera

The iPad doesn't include a USB port or SD memory card slot, which happen to be the most popular methods for getting pictures (and videos) from a digital camera onto a computer. (Luckily, every iPad since the iPad 2 sports two cameras.)

All the same, the iPad delivers a marvelous photo viewer. That's why if you take a lot of pictures, Apple's camera connection accessories are worth considering. The $29 Camera Connection Kit for iPads with a 30-pin dock connector consists of the two components shown in Figure 8-1, either of which plugs into the 30-pin connector at the bottom of the iPad. One sports a USB interface that you can use with the USB cable that came with your camera to download pictures. The other is an SD Card Reader that lets you insert the memory card that stores your pictures. For iPads with Lightning connectors, you can buy a cable with an SD card reader or a cable that's a USB connector. Each is sold separately for $29.

Though the official line from Apple is that this USB adapter is meant to work with the USB cable from your digital camera, we tried connecting other devices. We got an old Dell USB keyboard to work with it. There's a possibility other devices will work too, including readers for non–SD-type memory cards, USB speakers, and more. But don't expect all your USB devices to be compatible because of the power requirements of those devices, and the fact that the requisite software drivers and such aren't loaded on the iPad.

We only hope that despite this helpful accessory, Apple will get around to adding USB to a future iPad model.

Figure 8-1: You have two ways to import images using the iPad Camera Connection Kit.

Connecting to a TV or Projector

The iPad has a pretty big screen for what it is, a tablet computer. But that display is still not nearly as large as a living room TV or a monitor you might see in a conference room or auditorium.

Projecting what's on the iPad's screen to a larger display is the very reason behind the iPad Digital AV Adapter cable that Apple is selling for $39. You can use it to connect your iPad to TVs, projectors, and HDMI-capable (High-Definition Multimedia Interface) displays. What for? To watch videos, slideshows, and presentations on the big screen.

This HDMI connection provides 1080p HD resolution for apps and presentations, and up to 720p for movies.

If you'd like to dispense with the cables altogether, iOS 5 (and later) includes *video mirroring* through AirPlay, enabling you to wirelessly display what you see on your iPad to a TV, projector, or HDMI display. There's one catch: That TV or display device has to be connected to an Apple TV that supports AirPlay.

Keeping a Spare Charger

With roughly 10 hours of battery life, a single charge can more than get you through a typical workday with your iPad. But why chance it? Having a spare charger at the office can spare you (!) from having to commute with one. The Apple iPad 10W USB Power Adapter goes for $29 and includes a lengthy 6-foot cord.

Listening and Talking with Headphones

You've surely noticed that your iPad did not include earphones or a headset. Apple offers the standard iPod earphones (with remote and microphone) separately for the iPad at a reasonable $29.

Naturally, you also have an opportunity to select a pair of headphones, earphones, or a headset that suits your needs and your budget.

Wired headphones, earphones, and headsets

Search Amazon.com for headphones, earphones, or headsets and you'll find thousands available at prices ranging from around $10 to more than $1,000. Or if you prefer to shop in a brick-and-mortar store, Target, Best Buy, and the Apple Store all have decent selections, with prices starting at less than $20.

With so many brands and models of earphones, headphones, and headsets available from so many manufacturers at so many price points, we can't possibly test even a fraction of the ones available today. That said, we've probably tested more of them than most people have, and we have our favorites.

For earphones and earphone-style headsets, consider the Image S4 Headphones and S4i In-Ear Headset with Mic and 3-Button Remote, both from Klipsch. At around $79 and $99, respectively, they sound better than many similarly priced products and better than many more expensive offerings.

Bluetooth stereo headphones, earphones, and headsets

The idea behind Bluetooth stereo headphones/earphones/ headsets is simple: You can listen to music wirelessly up to 33 feet away from your iPad. If this sounds good to you, we suggest that you look for reviews of such products on the web before you decide which one to buy. A good place to start is Amazon.com, where we found more than 300 stereo Bluetooth headsets, with prices starting as low as $15.

Listening with Speakers

You can connect just about any speakers to your iPad, but if you want decent sound, we suggest you look only at *powered* speakers and not *passive* (unpowered) ones. The difference is that powered speakers contain their own amplification circuitry and can deliver much better (and louder) sound than unpowered speakers.

Prices range from less than $100 to hundreds (or even thousands) of dollars. Most speaker systems designed for use with your computer, iPod, or iPhone work well as long as they have an Aux input or a dock connector that can accommodate your iPad. (We haven't seen any with the dock connector yet, but, surely, some will be available soon.)

Desktop speakers

Logitech (www.logitech.com) makes a range of desktop speaker systems priced from less than $25 to more than $300. Logitech makes a variety of decent systems at a wide range of price points. If you're looking for something inexpensive, you can't go wrong with most Logitech-powered speaker systems.

Bluetooth speakers

Like Bluetooth headsets, Bluetooth speakers let you listen to music up to 33 feet away from your iPad. They're great for listening by the pool or hot tub or anywhere else that you might not want to take your iPad.

Docking your iPad with an extender cable

Because of its much larger size compared to an iPod or iPhone, you can't just dock the iPad into a speaker system designed for the smaller devices. All is not lost if you're partial to those speakers and still want to connect the iPad. CableJive (cable-jive.com) sells a dockXtender cable that enables you to dock your iPad from a distance; it's described as a 30-pin Male to Female Extension cable. Versions come in black and two standard lengths: $25.95 for a 2-foot length and $31.95 for 6 feet.

If your iPad has a Lightning connector, Apple's compact or cabled Lightning to 30-pin adapter enables you to dock your iPad to 30-pin accessories. We expect to see more Lightning-compatible accessories on the market soon.

But Wait . . . There's More!

Before we leave the topic of accessories, we think you should know about a few more products, namely film protection products that guard your iPad's exterior (or screen) without adding a bit of bulk and the Griffin Technology A-Frame table-top stand for your iPad.

Protecting the screen with film

Some people prefer not to use a case with their iPads, and that's okay. But if you're one of those people (or even if you're not), you might want to consider protective film for the iPad screen or even the whole device. We've tried these products on our iPhones in the past and have found them to perform as promised. If you apply them properly, they're nearly invisible and protect your iPad from scratches and scrapes without adding any bulk.

Manufacturers of film protectors include Zagg (www.zagg.com), BodyGuardz (www.bodyguardz.com), and Best Skins Ever (www.bestskinsever.com).

Any or all of the "skins" can be tricky to apply. Follow the instructions closely, watch videos on the vendors' websites and YouTube, and take your time. If you do, you'll be rewarded with clear film protection that is nearly invisible yet protects your iPad from scratches, nicks, and cuts.

One last thing: RadTech (www.radtech.us) offers two types of ClearCal Mylar screen protectors — clear transparent and anti-glare. These screen protectors are somewhat stiffer than the film products, and unlike film, they can be cleaned and reapplied multiple times with no reduction in performance. They effectively hide minor scratches, surface defects, and abrasions; and the hard Mylar surface not only resists scratches and abrasions but also is optically correct. Finally, they're reasonably priced at $19.95 for a pair of protectors of the same type.

Standing up your iPad with Griffin A-Frame

The Griffin A-Frame ($49.99) is so unusual we just had to include it. As you can see in Figure 8-2, it's a dual-purpose desktop stand made of heavy-duty aluminum. You can open it to hold your iPad in either portrait or landscape mode for video watching, displaying pictures (a great way to exploit the Picture Frame mode), or even reading. In this upright mode, it's also the perfect companion for the Apple Wireless Keyboard (or any other Bluetooth keyboard for that matter). Or close the legs and lay it down, and it puts your iPad at the perfect angle for using the onscreen keyboard.

Photos courtesy of Griffin Technology

Figure 8-2: The Griffin A-Frame is a unique, dual-purpose tabletop stand for your iPad.

Soft silicone padding keeps your iPad from getting scratched or sliding around, and the bottom lip is designed to accommodate the charging cable in portrait mode. Furthermore, it works with many third-party cases, including Griffin's flexible and hard-shell cases, among others.

Chapter 9

Ten Hints, Tips, and Shortcuts

*A*fter spending a lot of quality time with our iPads, it's only natural that we've discovered more than a few helpful hints, tips, and shortcuts. In this chapter, we share some of our faves.

Sliding for Accuracy

Our first tip is about a technique we call the *slide*. It can help you type faster in two ways: It helps you type more accurately, and it lets you type punctuation and numerals faster.

Start by performing the first half of a tap. That is, touch your finger to the screen but don't lift it. Now, without lifting your finger, slide it onto the key you want to type. You'll know you're on the right key because it changes from one shade of gray to another.

First, try the slide during normal typing. Stab at a key and if you miss, rather than lifting your finger, backspacing, and trying again, do the slide onto the proper key. After you get the hang of it, you'll see that it saves a lot of time and improves your accuracy as well.

Now here's the best part: You can use the slide to save time with punctuation and numerals, too. The next time you need to type a punctuation mark or number, start a slide action with your finger on the 123 key. When the punctuation and numeric keyboard appears, slide your finger onto the mark or number you want to type and then lift your finger. The cool thing is that the punctuation and numeric keyboard disappears, and the alphabetical keyboard reappears — all without tapping the 123 key to display the punctuation and numeric keyboard and without tapping the ABC key.

Using the Autoapostrophe

First, before moving on from the subject of punctuation, you should know that you can type **dont** to get to **don't**, and **cant** to get to **can't**. We've told you to put some faith in the iPad's autocorrection software. And that applies to contractions. In other words, save time by letting the iPad's intelligent keyboard insert the apostrophes on your behalf for these and other common words.

We're aware of at least one exception. The iPad cannot distinguish between *it's,* the contraction of *it is,* and *its,* the possessive adjective and possessive pronoun.

In a similar vein, if you ever *need* to type an apostrophe (for example, when you want to type *it's*), you don't need to visit the punctuation and numeric keyboard. Instead, press the Exclamation Mark/Comma key for at least one second and an apostrophe magically appears. Slide your finger onto it and then lift your finger, and presto — you've typed an apostrophe without touching the punctuation and numeric keyboard.

Viewing the iPad's Capacity

When your iPad is selected in the sidebar in iTunes, you see a colorful chart at the bottom of the screen that tells you how your iPad's capacity is being used by your media and other data.

By default, the chart shows the amount of space that your audio, video, and photo files use on your iPad in megabytes (MB) or gigabytes (GB). When you click any of the file headings beneath the colorful chart, it cycles through two more slightly different displays. The first click changes the display from the amount of space used to the number of items (audio, video, and photos) you have stored. Click once more and the display changes to the total playing time for audio and video, as shown in Figure 9-1.

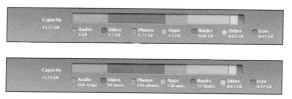

Figure 9-1: Click the colorful chart, and what's stored on your iPad is expressed in different ways.

Changing the Scrubber Speed

You're listening to a podcast or audiobook and want to find the beginning of a specific segment by moving the Scrubber left and right. With your finger on the Scrubber (that little round dot on the Scrubber bar), you can slide your finger to the left or right, and downward toward the bottom of the screen. If you slide left or right, the default (normal) scrubbing speed is called hi-speed scrubbing. When you slide your finger downward an inch or two, the speed changes to half-speed scrubbing. Drag another inch or two and it changes to quarter-speed scrubbing. Drag downward to near the bottom of the screen and it changes to fine scrubbing.

While you're scrubbing, keep an eye on the elapsed and remaining time indicators because they provide useful feedback on the current scrubbing speed.

The Scrubber in the iOS 5 (or later) Music app is a little harder to manipulate than the Scrubber bubble in iOS4's iPod app, which had a bigger, rounder Scrubber that was easier to grab. The secret in iOS 5 (or later) is to make sure that you've grabbed the Scrubber by pressing it and sliding your finger to the left or right. If the elapsed and remaining time changes when you slide, you're good to go.

Exploring Some Safari Tricks

The iPad does something special when it encounters an e-mail address or a URL in e-mail messages. It interprets character sequences that look like web addresses (URLs), such as `www.WebSiteName.com`, and any sequences that look like e-mail addresses, such as `YourName@YourMailHost.com`. When the iPad sees what it assumes to be a URL or e-mail address, it appears as a blue link on your screen.

If you tap a URL or e-mail address like the ones just shown, the iPad launches Safari and takes you to the appropriate web page for a URL, or starts a new e-mail message for an e-mail address.

Here's another cool Safari trick, this time with links. If you press and hold a link rather than tapping it, a little floating text bubble appears and shows you the underlying URL. In addition it offers four options:

- **Open:** Opens the page.

- **Open in New Tab:** Opens the page while stashing the current page in a separate tab.

- **Add to Reading List:** Adds the underlying URL to your Safari Reading List for later perusal.

- **Copy:** Copies the URL to the Clipboard (so that you can paste it into an e-mail message, save it in Notes, or whatever).

Finally, here's one last Safari trick. If you press and hold on most images, the Save Image and Copy buttons appear. Tap Save Image and the picture is saved to the Saved Photos album in the Albums tab of the Photos app; tap Copy and it's copied to the Clipboard.

Sharing the Love

Ever stumble on a web page you just have to share with a buddy? The iPad makes it dead simple, using a veritable host of options! From the site in question, tap the action button at the top of the browser (which looks like a square sprouting a curved arrow).

Your first sharing option is a Mail message. Tap the Mail button and a mail message appears with the subject line pre-populated with the name of the website you're visiting, and the body of the message pre-populated with the URL. Just type something in the message body (or don't), supply your pal's e-mail address, and tap the Send button.

The Action button also sports buttons for Twitter and Facebook — tap either button and you can immediately begin typing the body of your Twitter tweet or Facebook post. Again, the URL is included automatically.

Finally, tap Message to create a new text message with the URL, ready for you to address.

Choosing a Safari Home Page

You may have noticed that there's no home page website on the iPad version of Safari as there is in the Mac and PC versions of the browser. Instead, when you tap the Safari icon, you return to the last site you visited. The trick is to create an icon for the page you want to use as your home page. This technique is called creating a *web clip* of a web page. You simply open the web page you want to use as your home page and tap the action button. Then, tap the Add to Home Screen button. An icon appears on the next screen with an available spot. Tap this new icon instead of the Safari icon, and Safari opens to your home page.

Storing Files

Ecamm Network sells an inexpensive piece of Mac OS X software that lets you copy files from your Mac to your iPad and from the iPad to your Mac. (No Windows version is available.) You can try the $29.95 program called PhoneView for a week before deciding whether you want to buy it. Go to www. ecamm.com to fetch the free demo.

Making Phone Calls

You *can* make and receive phone calls on your iPad. After all, two of the key components to calling are built into the iPad: a speaker and microphone. Now all you have to do is head to the App Store to fetch a third component: an app that takes advantage of what's known as VoIP (Voice over Internet Protocol). In plain-speak, that means turning the iPad into a giant iPhone. We've checked out Skype, Toktumi's Line2, and Truphone, all of which are native iPad apps. The apps themselves are free, although you have to pay for calls to regular phones.

Snapping a Shot of the Screen

If you ever need a quick shot of what's showing on the iPad screen, here is how you do it. Press the Sleep/Wake button at the same time you press the Home button, but just for an instant. You'll hear the camera click, and the iPad grabs a snapshot of whatever is on the screen. The picture lands in the Camera Roll album in the Albums tab of the Photos app; from there, you can synchronize it with your PC or Mac, along with all your other pictures, or e-mail it to yourself or anyone else.

Index